75 20-MINUTE RECIPES

75 20-MINUTE RECIPES

HOW TO RUSTLE UP TEMPTING DISHES IN HARDLY ANY TIME: FABULOUS RECIPES FOR EVERY OCCASION SHOWN STEP BY STEP IN OVER 350 EASY-TO-FOLLOW PHOTOGRAPHS

JENNI FLEETWOOD

HERMES HOUSE

This edition is published by Hermes House, an imprint of Anness Publishing Ltd, Hermes House,
88–89 Blackfriars Road, London SE1 8HA; tel. 020 7401 2077; fax 020 7633 9499

www.hermeshouse.com; www.annesspublishing.com

If you like the images in this book and would like to investigate using them for publishing, promotions or advertising, please visit our website www.practicalpictures.com for more information.

Publisher: Joanna Lorenz
Managing Editor: Linda Fraser
Editor: Joy Wotton
Designers: Nigel Partridge and Ian Sandom
Photography: Karl Adamson, Steve Baxter, William Lingwood, Patrick McLeavey and Tom Odulate
Recipes: Alex Barker, Kit Chan, Christine France, Sarah Gates, Shirley Gill, Soheila Kimberley, Elisabeth Lambert Ortiz, Maggie Pannell and Hilaire Walden

ETHICAL TRADING POLICY
Because of our ongoing ecological investment programme, you, as our customer, can have the pleasure and reassurance of knowing that a tree is being cultivated on your behalf to naturally replace the materials used to make the book you are holding. For further information about this scheme, go to www.annesspublishing.com/trees

© Anness Publishing Ltd 2003, 2011

All rights reserved. No part of this publication may be reproduced, stored in a retrieval system, or transmitted in any way or by any means, electronic, mechanical, photocopying, recording or otherwise, without the prior written permission of the copyright holder.

A CIP catalogue record for this book is available from the British Library.

Previously published as *Tasty Meals in 20 Minutes*

NOTES
Bracketed terms are intended for American readers.
For all recipes, quantities are given in both metric and imperial measures and, where appropriate, in standard cups and spoons.
Follow one set of measures, but not a mixture, because they are not interchangeable.
Standard spoon and cup measures are level. 1 tsp = 5ml, 1 tbsp = 15ml, 1 cup = 250ml/8fl oz.
Australian standard tablespoons are 20ml. Australian readers should use 3 tsp in place of 1 tbsp for measuring small quantities.
American pints are 16fl oz/2 cups. American readers should use 20fl oz/2.5 cups in place of 1 pint when measuring liquids.
Electric oven temperatures in this book are for conventional ovens. When using a fan oven, the temperature will probably need to be reduced by about 10–20°C/20–40°F. Since ovens vary, you should check with your manufacturer's instruction book for guidance.
Medium (US large) eggs are used unless otherwise stated.
Main front cover image shows Sweet-and-sour Pork, Thai-style – for recipe, see page 44.

PUBLISHER'S NOTE
Although the advice and information in this book are believed to be accurate and true at the time of going to press, neither the authors nor the publisher can accept any legal responsibility or liability for any errors or omissions that may have been made nor for any inaccuracies nor for any loss, harm or injury that comes about from following instructions or advice in this book.

CONTENTS

Almost Instant *6*

Shopping for Short Cuts *8*

Equipment *10*

Quick-cooking Techniques *12*

Mix and Match Menus *14*

20-MINUTE RECIPES *16*

Soups, Appetizers and Snacks *18*

Poultry and Meat *36*

Fish and Shellfish *50*

Vegetarian Dishes *70*

Pasta and Rice *82*

Desserts *88*

Index *96*

ALMOST INSTANT

Twenty minutes. It isn't long, is it? Unless you are clock-watching or waiting in the rain for a bus. Of course, when you're enjoying yourself, 20 minutes whips by. In the kitchen, time is equally elastic – 20 minutes is an age when you are hungrily waiting for a batch of biscuits to cool, but a mere moment when you need to get a meal on the table quickly because everyone is going out.

At such times, the temptation is to snatch a ready-made meal or open a can or two, but, while there's nothing wrong with serving convenience food occasionally, it makes much more sense in terms of finance and nutrition to cook something fresh.

Can you really cook a meal in just 20 minutes? Yes, you can. This book contains a superb collection of over 70 recipes, from soups, appetizers and time-saving snacks, through satisfying main courses to delicious desserts, all chosen for the speed with which they can be prepared and cooked.

Of course, precisely how long each dish will actually take to prepare depends on a number of factors including the competence of the cook and the inevitable distractions (pets, partners, children). Some dishes benefit from being chilled or marinated, but if time is short, skip these options.

Preparation and cooking times for each recipe are given as a guide. Where these are inextricably linked, as when the cook puts on a pan of pasta, then uses the time while it cooks to prepare the vegetables for a sauce, for instance, a combined time is given.

Planning

You don't get to be a fast food expert by standing in the middle of the kitchen and wondering what to cook. If you really do have only a very short time to make a meal, you need to be highly organized. This means planning the menu in advance, making sure you have all the ingredients and – if possible – doing some preparation ahead of

Above: This quick and simple Spanish Garlic Soup is prepared in moments and makes a great starter or light lunch.

time. If you're new to cooking, don't attempt a three-course meal at the outset. Or, if you do, choose a bought appetizer like a carton of Stilton and celery soup or something simple like hummus and crudités (both of which can be bought from a good supermarket). There's no law that says you can't buy the dessert, too – the best French cooks do it all the time – so pop into a patisserie and pick up a glazed fruit tart. Alternatively, buy an apple pie or chocolate cake from your local market or store. Another easy dessert is ice cream. Whisk a little of your favourite liqueur into good quality vanilla ice cream, or ripple it with home-made raspberry jam. Fresh fruit is always acceptable, too, but make sure each variety you buy is ripe and ready for eating.

Left: A well-stocked kitchen will help you get organized quickly when you are cooking in a hurry. Keep a good supply of dried pulses and canned and bottled goods.

That just leaves the main course. Choose something simple you know you can cope with, such as Summer Tuna Salad or Cod Creole. If you're a novice, these are ideal, as they don't need any accompaniments other than a loaf of really good bread. As you become more confident, you can attempt dishes like Beef Strips with Orange and Ginger, or Pork with Marsala and Juniper. Either of these are good with buttered noodles, which are very easy to cook alongside the main dish. As to vegetables for quick meals, the best advice is to keep them simple. Some lightly blanched fine green beans, steamed carrots and grilled baby tomatoes would be fine, and there's nothing wrong with frozen peas, especially if you toss them with a little shredded lettuce softened in butter.

Having decided what you are going to cook, check your refrigerator and pantry to see which provisions you need. Read the recipe carefully and make sure you've got the requisite equipment, too. These recipes don't require much by way of elaborate utensils, but if you need a food processor or an electric whisk and haven't got one, you could be in bother.

Even if you are not by nature an organized person – and have no ambition to become one – it can be helpful to plan meals for several days ahead. That way, the half cabbage left over from Monday's main dish can be used in soup on Wednesday, or the chunk of Parmesan bought for grating on tonight's pasta can also furnish curls for tomorrow's salad.

GETTING READY
If you're as short of time for shopping as you are for cooking, try to get everything you need from one place. To save even more time, write your shopping list logically, more or less as you are likely to encounter the ingredients. There's nothing more irritating than getting all the way round a supermarket only to see that you have forgotten the onions at the bottom of your list and have to go back for them.

Once you get home, the secret of successful quick cooking is to get all the ingredients and equipment ready, in the order in which they are to be used, television-cook fashion. Taking a few minutes to do this at the outset will save you a lot of time during the actual cooking. It is also safer, as you won't be leaving a pan of hot fat to find the spatula. Read the recipe through one last time before starting to cook and make sure you know exactly what is required.

COOKING SEVERAL COURSES
Having mastered the 20-minute dish, it is time to try the next challenge – the 20-minute menu. To make this easier, at the start of this book there are some

Left: Choose Beef Strips with Orange and Ginger and oodles of noodles for a fast and nutritious meal.

Above: Good quality lamb chops cook in a flash and are delicious served with a fresh mint vinaigrette and crisp sautéed potatoes.

suggestions for simple mix-and-match menus, either using recipes supplied here, or techniques for which no actual recipe is required. All these three- or four-course meals can be made in less than half an hour, although you might need to call for reinforcements if your deadline is inflexible.

HOME HELP
Calling for reinforcements is a good idea in any event. The idea that one person should be responsible for all the cooking in a household is hopelessly outdated. Cooking together is great fun, as long as each of you accepts there's more than one way to chop an onion or peel a pear. Some children enjoy cooking from a very young age. Older children and teenagers will not only acquire useful skills but a sense of achievement from their ability to feed their friends and families. Find out here how every quick cook can produce fast and fantastic food in just 20 minutes.

SHOPPING FOR SHORT CUTS

The canny cook cheats. Digging your own potatoes or picking and podding your own peas are both admirable pursuits, and the results are delicious, but for fabulous fast food what you really need is a first-class supermarket, which will do the hard work for you.

VEGETABLES AND FRUIT
It is now possible to buy a huge range of ready-to-cook vegetables and fruits, from trimmed beans and mangetouts (snow peas) to carrot batons and sliced leeks. Most types of fruit are easy enough to prepare, but look for ready-sliced fresh pineapple, mango and melon – fresh and tasty, without the fuss.

Salad leaves are available in astonishing variety – not cheap, but wonderfully convenient for the quick cook. In addition to iceberg, cos or romaine, radicchio and treviso lettuce, consider Little Gem, oakleaf and frisée. Also widely on sale are rocket (arugula), baby spinach leaves and lamb's lettuce. Another favourite leaf vegetable, especially in Britain, is watercress. To toss with your chosen salad, there is also a wide choice of ready-made dressings, including low-fat and fat-free versions. Garnish with croûtons, fried bacon or curls of Parmesan cheese.

If it is vegetable medleys you're after, you'll find them too. Packets of prepared mixed vegetables are on sale and, where once you would have been lucky to find a single stir-fry mix, there are now Thai, Chinese and other Asian mixtures. The stir-fry vegetables may come with a sauce so, for a quick main course, all you need do is stock up with strips of chicken, pork fillet (tenderloin) or steak.

CHILLED ITEMS
From the supermarket chiller cabinet, you'll want to buy fresh eggs, cream, crème fraîche, yogurt, cheeses, butter and margarine, and pastry. Look out for fresh pasta and pasta sauces, too. They not only taste superb, but cook to perfection in just a few minutes.

Above: Buy Parmesan cheese in the block. It keeps well and is wonderful for grating on pasta or rice dishes, or for creating curls as edible garnishes for salads.

MEAT
If meat is to be cooked very quickly, it has to be extremely tender. Turkey escalopes (US scallops) are ideal, especially if they are beaten out thinly, then crumbed or simply cooked in a tasty sauce. Liver (calf's or lamb's) is equally appropriate, and has the advantage of being an excellent source of iron. Chicken breast portions are useful in dozens of dishes, and pork fillet (tenderloin) stir-fries well. Steak is also a good choice for the speedy cook.

FISH
The original fast food, fish is also low in fat and easily digestible, making it ideal for all the family. Skinned fillets need no preparation and cook extremely quickly, as does shellfish.

CANS AND JARS
When speed is the determining factor, judicious use of canned goods can be invaluable. Dried beans, for instance, need to be soaked overnight and then cooked slowly before they become tender. Canned beans and chickpeas are

Below: The variety of fresh, washed salad leaves available makes it easy for the quick cook to make a colourful salad.

ready to use straight away, which means that you can prepare a range of vegetarian dishes and snacks in moments.

Once upon a time, canned tomatoes meant whole fruits in a thin, seed-laden liquid. Today the tomatoes are usually chopped, and you can get them with herbs, garlic, chopped (bell) peppers and chillies. Passata (bottled strained tomatoes) and puréed tomatoes, which are sold in jars and cans, are equally useful, as are the various types of tomato purée (paste).

Also invaluable are cans or jars of fruit, pimientos, artichoke hearts, pesto and olive tapenade. You'll also need several different types of oil and vinegar, and sauces of various kinds, including soy sauce, sweet chilli sauce, tomato ketchup and hoisin. Of course, some of these ingredients cost a little more, but convenience never came without a price.

Below: Canned beans are a great asset in the quick cook's kitchen. Just open the can, rinse and drain the contents and you've got the makings of all sorts of vegetarian dishes, salads and dips.

STAPLES

You'll need all the staples – flour, sugar, raising agents and rice. Don't forget short-grain varieties of rice like arborio and carnaroli, which are perfect for making risotto. Experiment with some of the newer flavours and shapes of pasta to add variety and interest to your meal. Ready-to-top pizza bases and tortillas or wraps save time and effort. and trifle sponges and slices of gingerbread are first steps to simple desserts.

FLAVOURINGS

Of course, if cooking is reduced to putting together assorted packages, it isn't very satisfying. The trick is to add extra ingredients of your own to give the dish a unique signature. Herbs, spices, sauces and aromatics such as fresh root ginger or lemon grass can make the difference between a dish that tastes as though it came off an assembly line and one that has everyone begging for the recipe.

USE YOUR FREEZER

For many people, the freezer is largely the place where they keep ready meals, but if you keep the right ingredients in it, you can transform them into quick meals almost as quickly as you can cook a frozen pizza or pie.

One of the most useful items is good stock. When you roast a chicken, save the carcass and boil it up with an onion, a leek, a couple of celery sticks and a bunch of parsley. When all the meat has fallen off the bones and the stock has a good flavour, drain it through a sieve or strainer into a large bowl. Taste it and adjust the seasoning. Then, cool the stock quickly and chill it. When it is cold, the fat will solidify and can be lifted off easily. Transfer it to plastic

Above: Thai fish sauce, Worcestershire sauce and anchovy essence are useful ways of enhancing the flavour of a dish in a flash.

tubs, leaving headspace to allow for expansion on freezing, and freeze for up to three months.

Other useful items for the quick cook are vegetables, especially frozen spinach, peas and beans, and fruit, especially raspberries, which thaw quickly and are ideal for quick desserts. Bananas, peeled, stuck on sticks and frozen until solid, make delicious quick desserts when dipped in chocolate sauce. Crêpes and pancakes are also worth freezing — savoury ones make tasty quick meals when filled with roasted vegetables or chicken in a sauce, while sweet pancakes are perfect for desserts.

Pitta breads are also useful for quick meals, either as containers or sliced in strips for serving with dips. Keep a few fancy breads (not too crusty, or they won't freeze well) for thawing and serving with soups or main courses.

Stock up wisely and cooking quick meals will be a cinch.

EQUIPMENT

Stocking up on every item in your local cookware shop will not make you a better or faster cook, but it is definitely worth investing in some good quality basic items. The right knife, the well-chosen pan, the efficient food processor can all save vital moments when you are trying to prepare a meal in just 20 minutes.

Pans

A few good pans in various sizes and with tight-fitting lids are a must. You will need at least one pan with a solid, heavy base, for food cooked with the minimum of fat that might otherwise scorch or burn.

A wok or deep-sided sauté pan is also very useful, especially if it is non-stick. If you have a limited budget, buy this first, as you can use it for all sorts of things, from stir-fries to sauced dishes. Food cooks faster when spread over a wide area, so a pan like this aids the quick cook. Woks come with either one handle or two, one handle is especially useful when stir-frying. Another useful item, which is very inexpensive, is the steamer basket. This compact little basket expands to fit most pans.

Above: Good quality heavy pans will help you cook fast without fear of burning or scorching the food.

Baking Dishes

If you are setting up a kitchen for the first time, buy a casserole that will serve six, even if there are only two of you. Remember that you are bound to entertain friends and family from time to time. Also, when making a curry or casserole, it is a good idea to cook double and freeze half for another meal. The most useful casseroles can be used on top of the stove as well as in the oven.

Shallow baking dishes are especially useful for potato gratin and roasting vegetables.

Knives

Good quality knives can halve your preparation time, but more importantly a really sharp knife is safer than a blunt one. You can do yourself a lot of damage if your hand slips when you are pressing down hard with a blunt knife.

For basic, day-to-day use, choose a good chopping knife or cook's knife, a small vegetable knife and a long, serrated bread knife. If you have the space, keep knives sharp by storing them in well-secured slotted racks. Storing knives in a drawer is not good for knives since the blades can easily become damaged when they are knocked around. If you do have to keep knives in a drawer, make sure they are stored with the handles towards the front for safe lifting, and keep the blades protected in some way. You could wrap each knife in a piece of bubble wrap, secured with an elastic band, for example.

Sharpen your knives regularly. A steel, which looks like a slim column of metal, is the traditional sharpening utensil, but the newer, small Swiss knife sharpeners, which look like squared off, miniature steels, also give a very good finish. Professional chefs tend to eschew electric knife sharpeners, which can grind down too much of the cutting surface.

Left: A wide selection of baking dishes means you always have the right size of dish to hand.

Above: Use a steel to keep knives and cleavers sharp the professional way, but handle them with care.

Equipment

Left: A sharp and efficient grater will save time.

Above: A balloon whisk will swiftly beat the lumps out of any sauce.

Graters
Look out for the latest flat stainless steel graters. These are extremely efficient, with rubber grips at the base to prevent slipping. They grate a wide variety of foods perfectly without clogging, but are incredibly sharp, so handle them with care.

Measuring
For measuring, you will need a good scale, preferably one with imperial and metric measures. Electronic scales are very accurate, but expensive. Also invest in a set of measuring spoons, which are calibrated in size from 1.5ml/¼ tsp to 15ml/1 tbsp.

When speed is of the essence and accurate measuring isn't essential, use American measuring cups. This cookbook gives American cup measures for many dry goods and liquids. However, because American measuring cups are not standardized, they are no substitute for the scale when accuracy is vital, as when making cakes.

Electrical Items
For the fast cook, a food processor is essential. It will chop, grate, slice, beat and mince ingredients in seconds. Look for one with a second, smaller bowl, which fits inside the larger one. This comes with its own mini blade and is perfect for small amounts, as when you want to make a few breadcrumbs. A food processor can also be used as a blender, but the results are not always entirely satisfactory. If you make a lot of soups and purées, then you will probably prefer to have a separate blender.

Small Utensils
Other pieces of essential equipment include chopping boards, a colander, a sieve or strainer, and a whisk. A balloon whisk is useful for whisking gravies, smoothing out lumps and bringing a gloss to sauces. If you've made a sauce in a hurry and it has a few lumps, take it off the heat and place it on a cold surface, such as the sink, and whisk furiously. The lumps will soon disappear. For speedy juicing of citrus fruits, use a reamer. This small old-fashioned utensil, which looks a little bit like a large wooden flower bud on the end of a stalk, is very efficient. It doesn't catch the seeds or pips, though, so juice fruit into a strainer placed over a jug or pitcher.

An essential for the fast cook is a slotted spoon. When cooking blanched vegetables and pasta, for instance, blanch the vegetables in boiling water, use the slotted spoon to lift them out, and then use the same water to cook the pasta.

Above: Measuring spoons and cups are often used by quick cooks.

Above: A food processor cuts down on time spent beating and chopping.

Quick-Cooking Techniques

Every quick cook needs a few basics that can be mixed and matched to make a meal in moments. In the savoury stakes, the prime candidate has to be home-made tomato sauce. Use it to top pasta or a scone pizza; mix it with sliced smoked sausages; or spoon it over grilled (broiled) steaks or chicken. Spice it up with chillies and serve topped with a fried egg or pour it over cauliflower, sprinkle with grated cheese and grill.

Quick Scone Pizza

Preparation time 10 minutes
Cooking time 20 minutes

SERVES 4–6
*115g/4oz/1 cup self-raising (self-rising) white flour
115g/4oz/1 cup self-raising (self-rising) wholemeal (whole- wheat) flour
pinch of salt
50g/2oz/¼ cup butter, diced
about 150ml/¼ pint/⅔ cup milk
1 quantity of tomato sauce (see right)
toppings of own choice*

1 Preheat the oven to 220°C/425°F/Gas 7. Mix the flours and salt in a bowl. Rub in the butter. Add the milk and mix to a dough.

2 Knead the dough gently until smooth, then roll it out and line a 30 x 18cm/12 x 7in Swiss roll tin (jelly roll pan), pushing up the edges to form a rim. Spread with the tomato sauce and add your favourite toppings. Bake for about 20 minutes.

Tomato Sauce

Preparation time 10 minutes
Cooking time 20 minutes

MAKES ABOUT 300ML/½ PINT/1¼ CUPS
*15ml/1 tbsp olive oil
1 onion, finely chopped
1 garlic clove, crushed
400g/14oz can chopped tomatoes
15ml/1 tbsp tomato purée (paste)
15ml/1 tbsp chopped fresh mixed herbs
pinch of sugar
salt and ground black pepper*

1 Heat the oil in a pan, add the onion and garlic and cook over a gentle heat for 5 minutes, stirring occasionally, until softened.

2 Add the tomatoes, then stir in the tomato purée, fresh mixed herbs, sugar and salt and ground black pepper to taste.

3 Bring to the boil, then simmer, uncovered, over a medium heat for about 15 minutes, stirring occasionally, until the mixture has reduced to a thick pulp. Leave to cool, then cover the sauce and chill until ready to use.

Cooking Pasta

Preparation time nil
Cooking time 3–12 minutes

SERVES 4
*350g/12oz pasta
salt
30ml/2 tbsp olive oil or a knob (pat) of butter, to serve*

1 Bring a large pan of lightly salted water to the boil. Add the pasta and stir to separate the strands or shapes.

2 Cook at a rolling boil until the pasta is tender but still firm to the bite. When halved, shapes must be cooked through.

3 Drain the pasta well in a colander, shaking it hard to remove the excess water. Tip into a bowl and add a drizzle of olive oil or a little butter and then sprinkle over a little grated Parmesan or add your favourite sauce.

Cook's Tip
Always cook pasta in plenty of water in a large pan to prevent it from sticking.

Three more great basics: pancakes can be served simply, with lemon and sugar, but are even tastier with chocolate sauce or raspberry purée, which can also be used to top ice cream, meringues or fruit. Raspberry purée is also delicious spooned over slices of brioche that have been soaked in egg and cream, then fried.

Perfect Pancakes

Preparation time 5 minutes
Cooking time 20 minutes

MAKES ABOUT 12
*175g/6oz/1½ cups plain
  (all-purpose) flour*
10ml/2 tsp caster (superfine) sugar
2 eggs
450ml/¾ pint/1¾ cups milk
25g/1oz/2 tbsp butter, melted

1 Sift the flour into a bowl and stir in the sugar. Make a well in the centre and add the eggs and half the milk. Stir, gradually incorporating the dry ingredients, until smooth, then beat in the remaining milk.

2 Stir most of the melted butter into the batter. Heat a pancake pan, then grease it lightly with butter. Spoon in about 60ml/4 tbsp of the batter, tilting the pan so it coats the base evenly. Cook until the pancake has set and small holes appear on the surface. Lift the edge; the base should be pale brown. Flip the pancake over. Cook the other side briefly. Slide out and keep hot while cooking more pancakes.

Chocolate Sauce

Preparation time 1 minute
Cooking time 5 minutes

MAKES 250ML/8FL OZ/1 CUP
*150ml/¼ pint/⅔ cup single
  (light) cream*
15ml/1 tbsp caster (superfine) sugar
*150g/5oz best quality plain
  (semisweet) chocolate, broken*
30ml/2 tbsp dark rum (optional)

1 Rinse out a small pan with cold water. This will help to prevent the sauce from catching on the base of the pan. Pour in the cream, stir in the sugar and bring to the boil over a medium heat.

2 Remove the pan from the heat and add the chocolate, a few pieces at a time, stirring after each addition until the chocolate has melted and the sauce is smooth. Stir in the rum, if using.

3 Pour the sauce into a jug (pitcher) and use immediately. Alternatively, pour it into a clean jar and cool quickly. Close the jar and store the sauce in the refrigerator for up to 10 days. Serve hot or cold.

Raspberry Purée

Preparation time 1–2 minutes
Cooking time 1–5 minutes

1 Hull, clean and dry fresh raspberries and place them in a blender or food processor. Pulse the machine a few times, scraping down the sides of the bowl once or twice, until the berries form a purée.

2 If using frozen raspberries, put them in a pan with a little sugar and place over a gentle heat to soften and release the juices. Simmer for 5 minutes, then cool.

3 Press the purée through a fine-mesh sieve to remove any fibres or seeds. Sweeten with a little icing (confectioners') sugar and sharpen the flavour with lemon juice or a fruit-flavour liqueur, to taste.

Cook's Tip
Other soft summer fruits can be used to make a purée, try strawberries or blueberries, which can be puréed raw, or peaches, apricots or nectarines, which should first be poached lightly.

MIX AND MATCH MENUS

You can produce a delicious meal in under 20 minutes if you mix and match. When deciding what to serve, choose at least one dish which can be left unattended for a time, during which you can put together a salad, appetizer or dessert. You can cut corners still further by using some bought items – like bags of crudités or prepared vegetables.

Teenagers' Treat

The bright red colour and spicy flavour make Red Pepper Soup with Chilli and Lime a winner with young people.

While the soup simmers, make Stilton Beefburgers. Preheat the grill so that the burgers can cook while the soup is being drunk.

Serve the burgers with a small side salad, or just a radicchio leaf tucked inside each bun.

For dessert, serve kiwi fruit in eggcups. Slice off the tops and supply small spoons.

Family Favourite

Everyone loves Corned Beef and Egg Hash. While it is cooking, make a Spinach and Beetroot Salad and cut up the pineapple.

Make the beetroot dressing and toss the salad while the eggs are poaching on top of the hash.

Pineapple Flambé is a refreshing quick and easy dessert since poaching the fruit only takes a moment. If you are serving this to small children, omit the brandy.

Good quality bought vanilla ice cream would be delicious with the pineapple.

Sophisticated Supper

Before you prepare Avocado and Papaya Salad, cook the garlic cloves for the pork dish in a large pan of water.

Pork with Marsala and Juniper is delicious. Serve with noodles, cooked in the garlicky pan.

Grilled Nectarines with Ricotta and Spice is such a simple dessert that it can be assembled during the final minutes of cooking the pork dish. Fill the nectarines and grill (broil) them while you eat the main course. Check them from time to time to make sure the topping is not burning.

MIX AND MATCH MENUS *15*

VEGETARIAN FEAST

For a special treat, start the meal with hot toasted Brioche with Mixed Mushrooms.

Tagliatelle with Tomatoes and Black Olives is very tasty. Make a salad while it cooks.

For a final flourish, make Orange Yogurt Brûlées. Assemble the dessert after serving the pasta, but do not add the sugar topping until you are ready to serve the salad.

Dress and serve the salad after the pasta. Top the desserts. Grill (broil) them while the salad is being eaten.

PARTY TIME

Always popular at a party, Mackerel and Apple Dip takes only a few minutes to make.

French Bread Pizzas with Artichokes are ideal for parties, as the tasty slices are just bitesize.

You don't need a recipe for this tasty snack. Just fry sliced chorizo sausage and onions in extra virgin olive oil for a few minutes. Toss them with chopped flat leaf parsley and offer cocktail sticks (toothpicks) as pick-ups.

Complete the party menu with bowls of toasted nuts and seeds.

LIGHT LUNCH

For an effortless appetizer, begin with Thai Prawn Salad with all the aroma of lemon grass.

Mixed Pepper Pipérade is perfect for a light lunch. Serve with hot buttered toast.

End the meal on a cheery note with Warm Pears in Cider. Cook the pears, remove them from the syrup and keep warm. Reduce the syrup while you finish cooking the pipérade.

Having served the dessert, offer a piece of Saint-Agur cheese with celery sticks and crackers.

20-MINUTE RECIPES

It may surprise you to find just how many delicious dishes can be prepared in 20 minutes. In less time than it takes to reheat a frozen meal, you can impress your guests with Poached Eggs with Spinach or Pan-steamed Mussels with Thai Herbs. Pasta really is faster these days, with fresh and quick-cook varieties readily available, so celebrate with Tagliatelle with Tomatoes and Black Olives. For a final flourish, try Apple Soufflé Omelette or Orange Yogurt Brûlées.

Fresh Tomato Soup with Cheese Croûtes

Intensely flavoured sun-ripened tomatoes need little embellishment in this fresh-tasting soup. If you buy from the supermarket, choose the ripest-looking ones and adjust the amount of sugar and vinegar, depending on the tomatoes' natural sweetness. On a hot day, this Italian soup is also delicious chilled.

Preparation time 5 minutes
Cooking time 13–14 minutes

SERVES 6

1.5kg/3–3½lb ripe tomatoes
400ml/14fl oz/1⅔ cups chicken stock
45ml/3 tbsp sun-dried tomato paste
30–45ml/2–3 tbsp balsamic vinegar
10–15ml/2–3 tsp caster (superfine) sugar
small handful fresh basil leaves, plus a few extra to garnish
salt and ground black pepper
toasted cheese croûtes and crème fraîche, to serve

1 Mark the tomatoes with a small cross at the base, plunge them into boiling water for 30 seconds, then refresh in cold water. Peel off the skins and quarter the tomatoes. Put them in a large pan and pour over the chicken stock. Bring just to the boil, reduce the heat, cover and simmer gently for about 10 minutes, or until all the tomatoes are pulpy.

2 Stir in the tomato paste, vinegar, sugar and basil. Season with salt and pepper, then cook gently, stirring, for 2 minutes.

3 Process the soup in a blender or food processor, then return to the pan and reheat gently.

4 Serve in heated bowls. Top each portion with one or two toasted cheese croûtes and a spoonful of crème fraîche, garnished with the basil leaves.

Cook's Tips
Use good-quality stock for this soup. If you don't have time to make your own stock – or feel that life's too short for such worthy pursuits – buy superior stock in a can or carton.

RED PEPPER SOUP WITH CHILLI AND LIME

The beautiful rich red colour of this soup makes it a very attractive appetizer or light lunch.

Preparation and cooking time 20 minutes

SERVES 4–6
4 red (bell) peppers, seeded and chopped
1 large onion, chopped
5ml/1 tsp olive oil
1 garlic clove, crushed
1 small red chilli, seeded and sliced
45ml/3 tbsp tomato purée (paste)
900ml/1½ pints/3¾ cups chicken stock
grated rind and juice of 1 lime
salt and ground black pepper
shreds of pared lime rind, to garnish

1 Cook the peppers and onion gently in the oil in a covered pan for about 5 minutes, shaking the pan occasionally.

2 Stir in the garlic, then add the chilli with the tomato purée. Stir in half the stock, then bring to the boil. Cover the pan, lower the heat and simmer for 10 minutes.

3 Purée the mixture in a food processor or blender. Return to the pan, then add the rest of the stock.

4 Add the grated lime rind and juice to the soup, with salt and pepper to taste. Bring the soup back to the boil, then serve immediately with strips of lime rind sprinkled into each bowl.

COOK'S TIPS
Yellow or orange (bell) peppers could be substituted for the red peppers. If you haven't got a fresh chilli (or don't have time to seed and slice one), add a dash or two of Tabasco sauce to the soup instead.

Spanish Garlic Soup

This is a simple and satisfying soup, made with one of the most popular ingredients in the quick cook's kitchen – garlic!

Preparation time 2 minutes
Cooking time 12 minutes

SERVES 4

30ml/2 tbsp olive oil
4 large garlic cloves, peeled
4 slices French bread, about 5 mm/¼in thick
15ml/1 tbsp paprika
1 litre/1¾ pints/4 cups beef stock
1.5ml/¼ tsp ground cumin
pinch of saffron threads
4 eggs
salt and ground black pepper
chopped fresh parsley, to garnish

1 Preheat the oven to 230°C/450°F/Gas 8. Heat the oil in a large pan. Add the whole garlic cloves and cook until golden. Remove and set aside. Fry the bread in the oil until golden, then set aside.

2 Add the paprika to the pan, and fry for a few seconds. Stir in the beef stock, cumin and saffron, then add the reserved garlic, crushing the cloves with the back of a wooden spoon. Season with salt and pepper, then cook for about 5 minutes.

3 Ladle the soup into four ovenproof bowls and break an egg into each. Place a slice of fried bread on top of each egg, then put the bowls in the oven for about 3–4 minutes, until the eggs are set. Sprinkle each portion with parsley and serve immediately.

COOK'S TIP
When you switch the oven on, put a baking sheet in at the same time. Stand the soup bowls on the hot baking sheet when you put them in the oven and you will be able to remove them quickly and easily as soon as the eggs have set.

FRESH PEA SOUP

You really need fresh peas for this soup, but podding them can be time-consuming. Delegate the job to young kitchen hands if you can, or use frozen peas, thawing and rinsing them before use.

Preparation time 2–5 minutes
Cooking time 15 minutes

SERVES 2–3
small knob (pat) of butter
2 or 3 shallots, finely chopped
400g/14oz/3½ cups shelled fresh peas
 (from about 1.4kg/3lb garden peas)
 or thawed frozen peas
475ml/16fl oz/2 cups water
45–60ml/3–4 tbsp whipping
 cream (optional)
salt and ground black pepper
croûtons or crumbled crisp bacon,
 to garnish

1 Melt the butter in a heavy pan or flameproof casserole. Add the shallots and cook for about 3 minutes, stirring occasionally.

COOK'S TIP
If you use frozen peas for the soup, cook them in flavoursome vegetable stock or light chicken stock instead of water, as they will lack the delicate flavour of freshly podded garden peas. Instead of stirring the cream into the soup, swirl it on top when serving.

2 Add the peas and water and season with salt and a little pepper. Cover and simmer for about 12 minutes for young or frozen peas and up to 15 minutes for large or older peas, stirring occasionally.

3 When the peas are tender, ladle them into a food processor or blender with a little of the cooking liquid and process until smooth.

4 Strain the pea soup into the pan or casserole, stir in the cream, if using, and heat through without boiling. Add seasoning and serve hot, garnished with croûtons or bacon.

HADDOCK AND BROCCOLI CHOWDER

A warming main-meal soup for hearty appetites.

Preparation time 5 minutes
Cooking time 15 minutes

SERVES 4

4 spring onions (scallions), sliced
450g/1lb new potatoes, diced
300ml/½ pint/1¼ cups water
300ml/½ pint/1¼ cups milk
1 bay leaf
225g/8oz/2 cups broccoli florets, sliced
450g/1lb smoked haddock fillets, skinned
200g/7oz can corn, drained
ground black pepper
chopped spring onions, to garnish

1. Place the spring onions and potatoes in a large pan and add the water, milk and bay leaf. Bring the liquid to the boil, then cover the pan, lower the heat and simmer gently for 8 minutes.

2. Add the broccoli. Cut the fish into bitesize chunks and add to the pan with the corn.

3. Season the mixture well with black pepper, then cover the pan and simmer for 5 minutes more, or until the fish is cooked through. Remove the bay leaf and sprinkle over the spring onions. Serve the soup hot, with crusty bread.

COOK'S TIPS
New potatoes are now available for most of the year. To save time, buy packs of ready-prepared new or salad potatoes, so all you have to do is dice them.

VARIATIONS
Smoked cod fillets would be equally good in this chowder, or, if you prefer, substitute white cod or haddock fillets for half or all of the smoked fish.

CORN AND CRAB CHOWDER

Chowder comes from the French word meaning a large cooking pot. This is what the fishermen on the east coast of North America used for boiling up whatever was left over from the sale of their catch for supper.

Preparation time 5 minutes
Cooking time 14 minutes

SERVES 4

25g/1oz/2 tbsp butter
1 small onion, chopped
350g/12oz can corn, drained
600ml/1 pint/2½ cups milk
175g/6oz can white crab meat, drained and flaked
115g/4oz/1 cup peeled, cooked prawns (shrimp)
2 spring onions (scallions), chopped
150ml/¼ pint/⅔ cup single (light) cream or creamy milk
pinch of cayenne pepper
salt and ground black pepper
4 cooked prawns in shells, to garnish

1. Melt the butter in a large pan and gently cook the onion for 4–5 minutes, until softened.

2. Reserve 30ml/2 tbsp of the corn for the garnish and add the remainder to the pan with the milk. Bring the milk to the boil, then lower the heat, cover the pan and simmer gently, stirring occasionally, for 5 minutes.

3. Pour the corn mixture, in batches if necessary, into a blender or food processor and process until smooth.

4. Return the mixture to the pan and stir in the crab meat, prawns, spring onions, cream or milk and cayenne pepper. Reheat gently.

5. Meanwhile, place the reserved corn kernels in a small frying pan without oil and dry-fry over a medium heat until golden and toasted. Season the soup well and serve each bowlful topped with a few of the toasted kernels and a whole prawn.

Chilli Beef Nachos

The addition of minced beef to this traditional appetizer demonstrates its use as an excellent extender, creating a filling, quick meal.

Preparation time 3–4 minutes
Cooking time 14–15 minutes

SERVES 4

225g/8oz/2 cups minced (ground) beef
2 red chillies, chopped
3 spring onions (scallions), chopped
175g/6oz nachos
300ml/½ pint/1¼ cups sour cream
50g/2oz/½ cup grated Cheddar cheese
salt and ground black pepper

1 Dry-fry the minced beef and chillies in a large pan for about 10 minutes, stirring constantly.

2 Add the spring onions, season well and cook for a further 2 minutes. Preheat the grill (broiler).

3 Arrange the nachos in four individual flameproof dishes.

4 Spoon on the beef mixture, top with spoonfuls of sour cream and sprinkle with the grated cheese. Grill (broil) under a medium heat for 2–3 minutes, until the cheese is bubbling. Serve immediately.

Breaded Sole Batons

Crisp, crumbed fish strips — almost as speedy but smarter than fish fingers.

Preparation time 10–12 minutes
Cooking time 6–7 minutes

SERVES 4
275g/10oz lemon sole fillets, skinned
2 eggs
115g/4oz/2 cups fresh breadcrumbs
75g/3oz/¾ cup plain (all-purpose) flour
salt and ground black pepper
oil, for frying
lemon wedges and tartare sauce, to serve

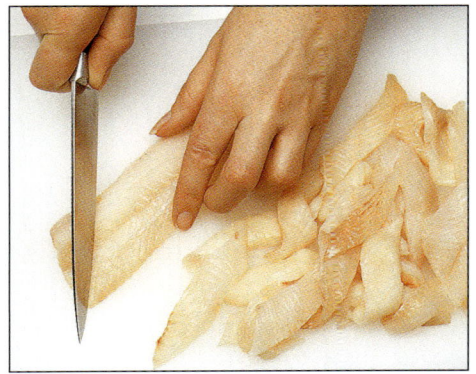

1 Cut the fish fillets into long diagonal strips each measuring about 2cm/¾in wide.

2 Break the eggs into a shallow dish and beat well with a fork. Place the breadcrumbs in another shallow dish. Put the flour in a large plastic bag and season with salt and ground black pepper.

3 Dip the fish strips in the egg, turning to coat well. Place on a plate and then shake a few at a time in the bag of seasoned flour. Dip the fish strips in the egg again and then in the breadcrumbs, turning to coat well. Place on a tray in a single layer, not touching. Let the coating set for at least 5 minutes.

4 Heat 1cm/½in oil in a large frying pan over a medium-high heat. When the oil is hot (a cube of bread will sizzle), fry the fish strips, in batches, for about 2–2½ minutes, turning once, taking care not to overcrowd the pan. Drain on kitchen paper and keep warm. Serve the fish with tartare sauce and lemon wedges.

Smoked Mackerel and Apple Dip

This quick, fishy dip is served with tasty, curried dippers.

Preparation time 5 minutes
Cooking time 10 minutes

SERVES 6–8

350g/12oz smoked mackerel fillets
1 eating apple, peeled, cored and cut into chunks
150ml/¼ pint/⅔ cup fromage frais (farmer's cheese)
pinch of paprika or curry powder
salt and ground black pepper
apple slices, to garnish

For the dippers
25g/1oz/2 tbsp butter, softened
5ml/1 tsp curry paste
4 slices white bread, crusts removed

1. Place the smoked mackerel in a food processor with the apple, fromage frais and seasonings.

2. Process for about 2 minutes or until the mixture is really smooth. Check the seasoning, then transfer to a small serving dish.

3. Preheat the oven to 200°C/400°F/Gas 6. To make the dippers, place the bread on a baking sheet. Blend the butter and curry paste; then spread over the bread.

4. Cook the bread in the oven for about 10 minutes, or until crisp and golden. Cut into fingers and serve immediately, with the mackerel dip, garnished with the apple slices.

Cook's Tip
Instead of using plain sliced bread, try other breads for the dippers – Italian ciabatta, wholemeal (whole-wheat), rye, or pitta breads would be excellent.

Baked Eggs with Tarragon

Traditional cocotte dishes or small ramekins are ideal for this recipe.

Preparation time 1 minute
Cooking time 10–11 minutes

SERVES 4

40g/1½oz/3 tbsp butter
120ml/4fl oz/½ cup double (heavy) cream
15–30ml/1–2 tbsp chopped fresh tarragon
4 eggs
salt and ground black pepper
fresh tarragon sprigs, to garnish

1. Preheat the oven to 180°C/350°F/Gas 4. Butter four small ramekins and warm in the oven.

2. Gently warm the cream. Sprinkle some tarragon into each dish, then spoon in some cream.

3. Carefully break an egg into each of the prepared ovenproof dishes, season the eggs with salt and pepper and spoon a little more of the cream over each of the eggs.

4. Add a small knob (pat) of butter to each dish and place them in a roasting pan. Pour in hot water to come halfway up the sides of the dishes. Bake for 8–10 minutes, until the whites are just set and the yolks still soft. Garnish with tarragon.

POACHED EGGS WITH SPINACH

This classic recipe dish can be served as an appetizer, but is also excellent for a light lunch or brunch.

Preparation time 2 minutes
Cooking time 12 minutes

SERVES 4
25g/1oz/2 tbsp butter
450g/1lb young spinach leaves
2.5ml/½ tsp vinegar
4 eggs
salt and ground black pepper

For the hollandaise sauce
175g/6oz/¾ cup butter, cut into small pieces
2 egg yolks
15ml/1 tbsp lemon juice
15ml/1 tbsp water
salt and ground white pepper

COOK'S TIP
Hollandaise sauce is quick and easy to make in a blender or food processor. If you like, you can make it an hour or two in advance and keep it warm in a wide-mouthed vacuum flask.

1 To make the hollandaise sauce, melt the butter in a small pan over a medium heat until it bubbles, then remove from the heat.

2 Put the egg yolks, lemon juice and water into a blender or food processor and process to blend. With the machine running, slowly pour in the hot butter in a thin stream. Stop pouring when you reach the milky solids at the base of the pan. When the sauce thickens, season and add more lemon juice if needed. Transfer the sauce to a bowl, cover and keep warm.

3 Melt the butter in a heavy frying pan over a medium heat. Add the spinach and cook until wilted, stirring occasionally. Season and keep warm.

4 To poach the eggs, bring a medium pan of lightly salted water to the boil and add the vinegar. Break an egg into a saucer and slide the egg into the water. Reduce the heat and simmer for a few minutes, until the white is set and the yolk is still soft. Remove with a slotted spoon and drain. Trim any untidy edges with scissors and keep warm. Cook the remaining eggs in the same way.

5 To serve, spoon the spinach on to warmed plates and make an indentation in each mound. Place the eggs on top and pour over a little hollandaise sauce. Serve the remaining hollandaise separately.

Asparagus with Orange Sauce

The white asparagus grown in France is considered a delicacy by many, although it doesn't have the intense flavour of the green. White and large green spears are best peeled before cooking.

Preparation time 2–3 minutes
Cooking time 15 minutes

SERVES 6
175g/6oz/¾ cup unsalted (sweet)
　butter, diced
3 egg yolks
15ml/1 tbsp cold water
15ml/1 tbsp fresh lemon juice
grated rind and juice of
　1 unwaxed orange, plus extra
　shreds of orange rind,
　to garnish
salt and cayenne pepper, to taste
30–36 thick asparagus spears

1 Melt the butter in a small pan over a low heat; do not boil. Skim off any foam, remove the pan from the heat and set aside.

2 In a heatproof bowl set over a pan of barely simmering water or in the top of a double boiler, whisk together the egg yolks, water, lemon juice and 15ml/1 tbsp of the orange juice. Season with salt. Place the pan or double boiler over a very low heat and whisk constantly until the mixture begins to thicken and the whisk begins to leave tracks on the base of the pan. Remove the pan from the heat.

3 Whisk in the melted butter, drop by drop until the sauce begins to thicken, then pour it in a little more quickly, leaving behind the milky solids at the base of the pan. Whisk in the orange rind and 30–60ml/2–4 tbsp of the orange juice. Season with salt and cayenne and keep warm, stirring occasionally

4 Cut off the tough ends from the asparagus spears and trim to the same length. If peeling, hold each spear gently by the tip, then use a vegetable peeler to strip off the peel and scales from just below the tip to the end. Rinse in cold water.

5 Pour water to a depth of 5cm/2in into a large deep frying pan or wok and bring to the boil over a medium-high heat. Add the asparagus and bring back to the boil, then simmer for 4–7 minutes, until just tender.

6 Carefully transfer the spears to a large colander to drain, then lay them on a dishtowel; pat dry. Arrange on a large serving platter or individual plates and spoon over a little sauce. Sprinkle the orange rind over the sauce and serve.

COOK'S TIP
This sauce is a kind of hollandaise and needs gentle treatment. If the egg yolk mixture thickens too quickly, remove from the heat and plunge the base of the pan or bowl into cold water to prevent the sauce from curdling. The sauce should keep over hot water for 1 hour, but don't let it get too hot.

Asparagus Rolls with Herb Butter Sauce

For a taste sensation, try tender asparagus spears wrapped in crisp filo pastry. The buttery herb sauce doesn't take long to make and is the perfect accompaniment.

Preparation time 5 minutes
Cooking time 8 minutes

SERVES 2
4 sheets of filo pastry
50g/2oz/¼ cup butter, melted
16 young asparagus spears, trimmed
mixed salad, to garnish

For the sauce
2 shallots, finely chopped
1 bay leaf
150ml/¼ pint/⅔ cup dry white wine
175g/6oz/¾ cup butter, melted
15ml/1 tbsp chopped fresh herbs
salt and ground black pepper
chopped chives, to garnish

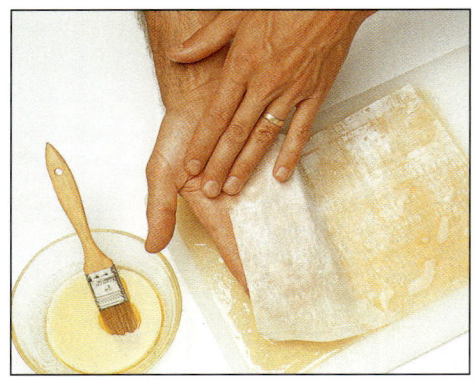

[1] Preheat the oven to 200°C/400°F/Gas 6. Grease a baking sheet. Brush each filo sheet with melted butter. Fold one corner of the sheet down to the bottom edge to give a wedge shape.

Cook's Tips
Make miniature asparagus rolls for parties. Cut smaller rectangles of filo and roll around a single asparagus spear. Serve hot, with the sauce, or cold, with a light mayonnaise. For a quicker and more economical version, use well-drained canned asparagus cuts, folding them inside filo envelopes.

[2] Lay 4 asparagus spears on top at the longest edge and roll up towards the shortest edge. Using the remaining filo and asparagus spears, make 3 more rolls in the same way.

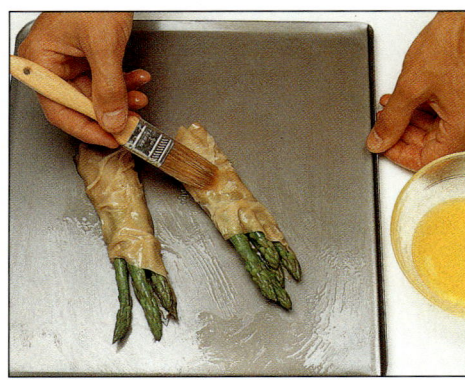

[3] Lay the rolls on the prepared baking sheet. Brush with the remaining melted butter. Bake for 8 minutes, until golden.

[4] Meanwhile, make the sauce. Put the shallots, bay leaf and wine into a pan. Cover and cook over a high heat until the wine is reduced to about 45–60ml/3–4 tbsp.

[5] Strain the wine mixture into a heatproof bowl. Whisk in the butter, a little at a time, until the sauce is smooth and glossy.

[6] Stir in the herbs and add salt and pepper to taste. Keep the sauce warm over a pan of barely simmering water. Serve the rolls on individual plates with the salad garnish. Serve the butter sauce separately, sprinkled with a few chopped chives.

Egg and Tomato Salad with Crab

Preparation time 5 minutes
Cooking time Nil

SERVES 4

1 round lettuce
2 x 200g/7oz cans
  crab meat, drained
4 hard-boiled eggs, sliced
16 cherry tomatoes, halved
½ green (bell) pepper, seeded and
  thinly sliced
6 pitted black olives, sliced

For the dressing
250ml/8fl oz/1 cup mayonnaise
10ml/2 tsp fresh lemon juice
45ml/3 tbsp chilli sauce
½ green (bell) pepper, seeded and
  finely chopped
5ml/1 tsp creamed horseradish
5ml/1 tsp Worcestershire sauce

[1] To make the dressing, place all the ingredients in a bowl and mix well. Set aside in a cool place.

[2] Line four plates with the lettuce leaves. Mound the crab meat in the centre. Arrange the eggs around the outside with the tomatoes on top.

[3] Spoon some of the dressing over the crab meat. Arrange the green pepper slices on top and sprinkle with the olives. Serve with the remaining dressing.

Summer Tuna Salad

This colourful salad is perfect for a summer lunch in the garden — use canned or freshly cooked salmon in place of the tuna, if you like.

Preparation time 20 minutes
Cooking time Nil

SERVES 4–6

175g/6oz radishes
1 cucumber
3 celery sticks
1 yellow (bell) pepper
175g/6oz cherry tomatoes, halved
4 spring onions (scallions),
  thinly sliced
45ml/3 tbsp fresh lemon juice
45ml/3 tbsp olive oil
2 x 200g/7oz cans tuna, drained
  and flaked
30ml/2 tbsp chopped fresh parsley
salt and ground black pepper
lettuce leaves, to serve
thin strips of twisted lemon rind,
  to garnish

[1] Cut the radishes, cucumber, celery and yellow pepper into small cubes. Place in a large, shallow dish with the cherry tomatoes and spring onions.

[2] Put the lemon juice in a bowl. Whisk in the oil, with salt and pepper to taste. Add the dressing to the vegetables, toss to coat, then set aside for 15 minutes.

[3] Add the flaked tuna and parsley to the mixture and toss gently until well combined.

[4] Arrange the lettuce leaves on a platter and spoon the salad into the centre. Garnish with the twisted lemon rind.

VARIATION
Prepare the vegetables as suggested in the recipe and add the chopped parsley. Arrange lettuce leaves on individual plates and divide the vegetable mixture among them. Place a mound of tuna on top of each and finish with a spoonful of mayonnaise.

SALADE NIÇOISE

Preparation and cooking time 20 minutes

SERVES 4

90ml/6 tbsp olive oil
30ml/2 tbsp tarragon vinegar
5ml/1 tsp tarragon or Dijon mustard
1 small garlic clove, crushed
115g/4oz green beans
12 small new or salad potatoes
3–4 Little Gem (Bibb) lettuces
200g/7oz can tuna in oil, drained
6 anchovy fillets, halved lengthways
12 pitted black olives
4 tomatoes, chopped
4 spring onions (scallions), chopped
10ml/2 tsp capers
30ml/2 tbsp pine nuts
2 hard-boiled eggs, chopped
salt and ground black pepper

1 Mix the oil, vinegar, mustard, garlic and seasoning with a wooden spoon in a large salad bowl.

COOK'S TIP
When buying the potatoes, pick the smallest ones you can find, so that they cook quickly.

2 Cook the green beans and potatoes in separate pans of salted, boiling water until just tender. Drain and add to the bowl with the lettuce, tuna, anchovies, olives, tomatoes, spring onions and capers.

3 Toast the pine nuts in a small frying pan over a medium heat until lightly browned.

4 Sprinkle the pine nuts over the salad while they are still hot, add the chopped hard-boiled eggs and toss all the ingredients together well. Serve immediately, with chunks of hot crusty bread.

Avocado and Papaya Salad

Preparation time 6–8 minutes
Cooking time Nil

SERVES 4
2 ripe avocados
1 ripe papaya
1 large orange
1 small red onion
25–50g/1–2oz small rocket (arugula) leaves or lamb's lettuce
For the dressing
60ml/4 tbsp olive oil
30ml/2 tbsp fresh lemon or lime juice
salt and ground black pepper

1. Halve the avocados and remove the stones (pits). Carefully peel off the skin, then slice each avocado half thickly.

2. Peel the papaya. Cut it in half lengthways and scoop out the seeds with a spoon. Set aside about 5ml/1 tsp of the seeds for the dressing. Cut each half into eight slices.

3. Peel the orange. Using a small sharp knife, cut out the segments, cutting either side of the dividing membranes. Slice the onion thinly and separate into rings.

4. Make the dressing. Combine the oil, lemon or lime juice and seasoning in a bowl and mix well. Stir in the reserved papaya seeds.

5. Assemble the salad on four individual serving plates. Alternate slices of papaya and avocado. Add the orange segments and a mound of rocket or lamb's lettuce topped with onion rings. Spoon over the dressing and serve.

Corned Beef and Egg Hash

This classic American hash is made with corned beef and is a popular brunch or lunchtime dish.

Preparation time 4 minutes
Cooking time 12–14 minutes

SERVES 4

30ml/2 tbsp sunflower oil
25g/1oz/2 tbsp butter
1 onion, finely chopped
1 small green (bell) pepper, seeded and diced
2 large boiled potatoes, diced
350g/12oz can corned beef, cubed
1.5ml/¼ tsp grated nutmeg
1.5ml/¼ tsp paprika
4 eggs
salt and ground black pepper
chopped fresh parsley, to garnish
sweet chilli sauce or tomato sauce, to serve

1. Heat the oil and butter together in a large frying pan and add the onion. Cook for 5–6 minutes, until softened.

2. In a bowl, mix together the green pepper, potatoes, corned beef, nutmeg and paprika and season well. Add to the pan and toss gently. Press down lightly and cook over a medium heat for about 3–4 minutes, until a golden brown crust has formed on the underside.

COOK'S TIP
Chill the corned beef before use – it will cut into cubes more easily.

3. Stir the hash mixture through to distribute the crust, then repeat the cooking twice, until the mixture is well browned.

4. Make four wells in the hash and crack an egg into each. Cover. Cook until the whites are just set.

5. Sprinkle with chopped parsley and cut the hash into quarters. Serve hot with sweet chilli sauce or tomato sauce.

STILTON BEEFBURGERS

Rather more up-market than the traditional beefburger, this recipe contains a delicious surprise. The lightly melted Stilton encased in this crunchy beefburger is delicious.

Preparation time 5 minutes
Cooking time 10 minutes

SERVES 4

450g/1lb/4 cups minced (ground) beef
1 onion, finely chopped
1 celery stick, chopped
5ml/1 tsp dried mixed herbs
5ml/1 tsp prepared mustard
50g/2oz/½ cup crumbled blue Stilton cheese
4 burger buns
salt and ground black pepper

1. Place the minced beef in a bowl together with the onion and celery. Season well.

2. Stir in the herbs and mustard, bringing the mixture together to form a firm mixture.

3. Divide the mixture into eight equal portions. Place four on a chopping board and flatten each one slightly to make patties.

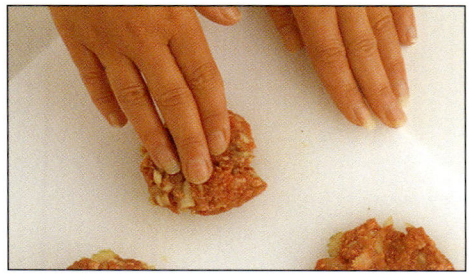

4. Place the crumbled cheese in the centre of each patty.

5. Flatten the remaining mixture and place on top. Mould the mixture together, encasing the crumbled cheese and shape into four burgers. Preheat the grill (broiler).

6. Grill (broil) under a medium heat for 10 minutes, turning once or until cooked through. Split the burger buns and place a burger inside each. Serve with salad and mustard pickle or tomato ketchup, if you like, although neither is essential, with the Stilton for flavouring.

Veal Kidneys with Mustard

In France, where this recipe originated, veal kidneys are easily found, but this dish is equally delicious made with lamb's kidneys.

Preparation time 5 minutes
Cooking time 10–12 minutes

Serves 4

*2 veal kidneys or 8–10 lambs'
   kidneys, trimmed and
   membranes removed*
25g/1oz/2 tbsp butter
15ml/1 tbsp vegetable oil
*115g/4oz/1 cup button (white)
   mushrooms, quartered*
60ml/4 tbsp chicken stock
30ml/2 tbsp brandy (optional)
*175ml/6fl oz/ 3/4 cup crème fraîche or
   double (heavy) cream*
30ml/2 tbsp Dijon mustard
salt and ground black pepper
chopped fresh chives, to garnish

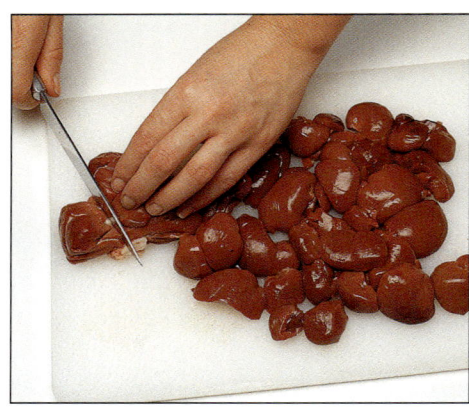

1. Cut the veal kidneys into pieces, discarding any fat. If using lambs' kidneys, remove the central core by cutting a V-shape from the middle of each kidney. Cut each kidney into three or four pieces.

Cook's Tip
Be sure not to cook the sauce too long once the mustard is added or it will lose its piquancy.

2. In a large frying pan, melt the butter with the oil over a high heat and swirl to blend. Add the kidneys and cook for 3–4 minutes, stirring frequently, until browned, then transfer them to a plate using a slotted spoon.

3. Add the mushrooms to the pan and cook for 2–3 minutes, until golden, stirring frequently. Pour in the chicken stock and brandy, if using, then bring to the boil and boil for 2 minutes.

4. Lower the heat, stir in the crème fraîche or double cream and cook for about 2–3 minutes, until the sauce is slightly thickened. Stir in the mustard and season with salt and pepper, then add the kidneys and cook for 1 minute to reheat. Spoon into a serving dish, sprinkle over the chives and serve.

Beef Strips with Orange and Ginger

Stir-frying is one of the quickest ways to cook, provided you choose tender meat.

Preparation time 15 minutes
Cooking time 5 minutes

SERVES 4

450g/1lb lean beef rump (round), fillet (tenderloin) or sirloin, cut into thin strips
grated rind and juice of 1 orange
15ml/1 tbsp light soy sauce
5ml/1 tsp cornflour (cornstarch)
2.5cm/1in piece of fresh root ginger, finely chopped
15ml/1 tbsp sunflower oil
1 large carrot, cut into thin strips
2 spring onions (scallions), sliced
noodles or rice, to serve

1. Place the beef strips in a bowl and sprinkle over the orange rind and juice. If possible, leave to marinate for 10 minutes, or up to 30 minutes if you can spare the time.

2. Drain the liquid from the meat and set aside, then mix the meat with the soy sauce, cornflour, and ginger.

3. Heat the oil in a wok or large frying pan and add the beef. Stir-fry for 1 minute until lightly coloured, then add the carrot and stir-fry for a further 2–3 minutes.

4. Stir in the spring onions and reserved liquid, then cook, stirring, until boiling and thickened. Serve hot with noodles or rice.

Cook's Tip
Just before serving, toss the stir-fry with 5ml/1 tsp sesame oil. If you haven't any sesame oil, use flavoured chilli oil, or a nut oil, such as hazelnut or walnut.

RAGOUT OF VEAL

Full of flavour, this is quick and easy. Use small cubes of pork fillet if you prefer.

Preparation time 3 minutes
Cooking time 17 minutes

SERVES 4

450g/1lb veal fillet (tenderloin)
30ml/2 tbsp olive oil
10–12 tiny onions, kept whole
1 yellow (bell) pepper, seeded and cut in eight
1 orange or red (bell) pepper, seeded and cut in eight
3 plum tomatoes, peeled and quartered
4 fresh basil sprigs
30ml/2 tbsp dry vermouth or sherry
salt and ground black pepper

1 Trim off any fat and cut the veal into cubes. Heat the oil in a frying pan and gently cook the veal and onions until browned.

2 After a couple of minutes add the peppers and tomatoes. Cook for a further 4 minutes.

3 Add half the basil leaves, coarsely chopped, the vermouth or sherry, and seasoning. Cook, stirring frequently, for 10 minutes, until the meat is tender.

4 Sprinkle with the remaining basil leaves and serve hot.

LAMB'S LIVER WITH PEPPERS

Tender and tasty lamb's liver can be cooked with all sorts of ingredients. Here it is matched with peppers and peppercorns.

Preparation time 7 minutes
Cooking time 3–4 minutes

SERVES 4

30ml/2 tbsp olive oil
2 shallots, sliced
450g/1lb lamb's liver, cut in thin strips
1 garlic clove, crushed
10ml/2 tsp green peppercorns, crushed (or more to taste)
½ red (bell) pepper, seeded and sliced
½ orange or yellow (bell) pepper, seeded and sliced
30ml/2 tbsp crème fraîche
salt and ground black pepper
rice or noodles, to serve

COOK'S TIP
Lamb's liver is best when still very slightly pink in the middle. Watch it closely as it soon overcooks.

1 Heat the oil and cook the shallots briskly for 1 minute. Add the liver, garlic, peppercorns and peppers, then stir-fry for 3–4 minutes.

2 Stir in the crème fraîche, season to taste and serve immediately with rice or noodles.

Lamb Chops with Mint Vinaigrette

Serving vinaigrette sauces with meat came in with nouvelle cuisine and stayed. This one offers a classic combination – lamb and mint – in a new style.

Preparation time 4 minutes
Cooking time 6–7 minutes

SERVES 4
8 loin lamb chops or 4 double loin chops, about 2cm/³⁄₄in thick
coarsely ground black pepper
fresh mint, to garnish
sautéed potatoes, to serve

For the mint vinaigrette
30ml/2 tbsp white wine vinegar
2.5ml/¹⁄₂ tsp clear honey
1 small garlic clove, very finely chopped
60ml/4 tbsp extra virgin olive oil
20g/³⁄₄oz/³⁄₄ cup fresh mint leaves, finely chopped
1 ripe plum tomato, peeled, seeded and finely diced
salt and ground black pepper

1 To make the vinaigrette, put the vinegar, honey, garlic, salt and pepper in a small bowl and whisk thoroughly to combine.

2 Slowly whisk in the oil, then stir in the mint and tomato and set aside.

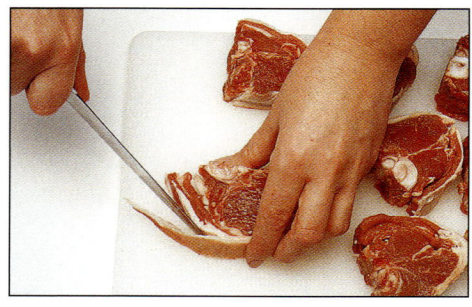

3 Put the lamb chops on a board and trim off any excess fat. Sprinkle with the pepper and press on to both sides of the meat.

4 Lightly oil a heavy cast iron griddle and set over a high heat until very hot but not smoking. Place the chops on the griddle and reduce the heat to medium. Cook the chops for 6–7 minutes, turning once, or until done as preferred (medium-rare meat will still be slightly soft when pressed, medium will be springy and well-done firm). Serve the chops with the vinaigrette and sautéed potatoes, garnished with mint.

Cook's Tip
The chops can also be cooked under a preheated grill (broiler) or on a barbecue until done as you like. If cooked on the barbecue, put them in a wire rack to make them easier to turn.

PORK WITH MARSALA AND JUNIPER

Although most frequently used in desserts, Sicilian Marsala gives savoury dishes a rich, fruity and alcoholic tang. Use good quality butcher's pork, which won't be overwhelmed by the intense flavour of the sauce.

Preparation time 4 minutes
Cooking time 15–16 minutes

SERVES 4

25g/1oz/½ cup dried cep or porcini mushrooms
4 pork escalopes (US scallops)
10ml/2 tsp balsamic vinegar
8 garlic cloves
15g/½oz/1 tbsp butter
45ml/3 tbsp Marsala
several fresh rosemary sprigs
10 juniper berries, crushed
salt and ground black pepper
noodles and green vegetables, to serve

1 Put the dried mushrooms in a bowl and just cover with hot water. Leave to stand.

2 Place the pork escalopes on a board, brush with 5ml/1 tsp of the vinegar and add a generous and even grinding of salt and black pepper. Bring a small pan of water to the boil and add the garlic cloves. Cook for 10 minutes, until softened. Drain well, put the garlic in a bowl and set aside while you cook the pork escalopes.

3 Melt the butter in a large frying pan. Add the pork and cook quickly until browned on the underside. Turn the meat over and cook for another minute.

4 Add the Marsala and rosemary to the pan. Drain the dried mushrooms, saving the juices, and add them to the mixture. Stir in 60ml/4 tbsp of the mushroom juices, then add the garlic cloves, juniper berries and remaining vinegar.

5 Simmer the mixture gently for about 3 minutes, until the pork is cooked. Season lightly and serve hot with noodles and vegetables.

COOK'S TIP
Juniper berries are the principal flavouring for gin. When added to meat, they impart a gamey flavour.

Sweet-and-Sour Pork, Thai-Style

Sweet and sour is traditionally a Chinese creation, but the Thais do it very well. This version has a clean, fresh flavour.

Preparation time 6 minutes
Cooking time 12–14 minutes

SERVES 4

350g/12oz lean pork
30ml/2 tbsp vegetable oil
4 garlic cloves, thinly sliced
1 small red onion, sliced
30ml/2 tbsp Thai fish sauce
15ml/1 tbsp granulated sugar
1 red (bell) pepper, seeded and diced
½ cucumber, seeded and sliced
2 plum tomatoes, cut into wedges
2 spring onions (scallions), cut into short lengths
115g/4oz pineapple, cut into small chunks
ground black pepper
fresh coriander (cilantro) leaves and shredded spring onions, to garnish

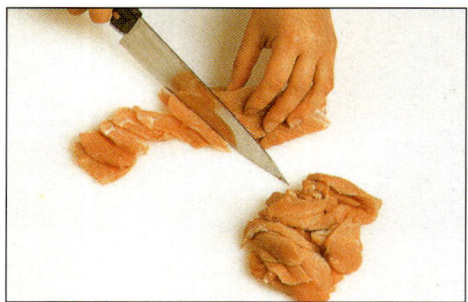

[1] Slice the pork into thin strips. Heat the oil in a wok or pan.

[2] Cook the garlic until golden, then add the pork and stir-fry for 4–5 minutes. Add the onion.

[3] Season the meat and onion mixture with fish sauce, sugar and ground black pepper. Stir the mixture (or toss it over the heat with two spoons or spatulas) for about 4 minutes, until the pork is cooked.

[4] Add the rest of the vegetables, with the pineapple. You may need to add a few tablespoons of water. Stir-fry for 3–4 minutes more. Serve hot, garnished with coriander leaves and spring onion.

Chicken Chow Mein

Chow Mein is arguably the best known Chinese noodle dish in the West.

Preparation time 4–5 minutes
Cooking time 14 minutes

SERVES 4

350g/12oz noodles
225g/8oz skinless, boneless chicken breast portions
45ml/3 tbsp soy sauce
15ml/1 tbsp rice wine or dry sherry
15ml/1 tbsp dark sesame oil
60ml/4 tbsp vegetable oil
2 garlic cloves, finely chopped
50g/2oz mangetouts (snow peas), trimmed
115g/4oz beansprouts
50g/2oz ham, finely shredded
4 spring onions (scallions), chopped
salt and ground black pepper

1. Cook the noodles in a large pan of lightly salted, boiling water until tender.

2. Meanwhile, slice the chicken into fine shreds about 5cm/2in in length. Place in a bowl and add 10ml/2 tsp of the soy sauce, the rice wine or sherry and sesame oil.

3. Heat half the vegetable oil in a wok or large frying pan over a high heat. When it starts smoking, add the chicken mixture. Stir-fry for 2 minutes, then transfer the chicken to a plate and keep it hot.

4. Wipe the wok clean and heat the remaining oil. Stir in the garlic, mangetouts, beansprouts and shredded ham. Stir-fry for 2–3 minutes more over a high heat.

5. Drain the noodles, rinse them under cold water, then drain them again. Pat them dry with kitchen paper and add to the wok. Continue to stir-fry until the noodles are heated through. Add the remaining soy sauce and season with salt and ground black pepper. Return the chicken and any juices to the noodle mixture, add the chopped spring onions and give the mixture a final stir. Serve immediately.

Caribbean Chicken Kebabs

These quick-to-cook kebabs have a rich, sunshine Caribbean flavour and the marinade keeps them moist without the need for oil.

Preparation time 12 minutes
Cooking time 8 minutes

SERVES 4
500g/1¼ lb skinless, boneless
  chicken breast portions
finely grated rind of 1 lime
30ml/2 tbsp lime juice
15ml/1 tbsp rum
15ml/1 tbsp light soft
  brown sugar
15ml/1 tsp ground cinnamon
2 mangoes, peeled and cubed
rice and salad, to serve

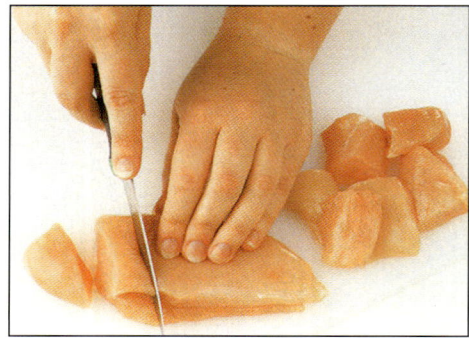

[1] Cut the chicken into bitesize chunks and place in a bowl with the lime rind and juice, rum, sugar and cinnamon. Toss well and set aside for 10 minutes.

[2] Drain the chicken, saving the juices and thread it on to four skewers, alternating with the mango cubes.

[3] Cook the skewers under a grill (broiler), or on a barbecue, for about 8 minutes, turning occasionally and basting with the juices, until the chicken is tender and golden brown. Serve the kebabs immediately, with rice and salad.

COOK'S TIP
The rum or sherry adds a lovely rich flavour to the marinade, but it can be omitted if you prefer to avoid the added alcohol.

VARIATIONS
Try using other fruits in place of the mangoes – chunks of fresh pineapple or firm peaches or nectarines would be equally good in this recipe.

Cajun-spiced Chicken

Preparation time 2 minutes
Cooking time 10–15 minutes

Serves 6

6 medium skinless boneless
  chicken breast portions
75g/3oz/⅓ cup butter
5ml/1 tsp garlic powder
10ml/2 tsp onion powder
5ml/2 tsp cayenne pepper
10ml/2 tsp paprika
1.5ml/¼ tsp ground cumin
5ml/1 tsp dried thyme
salt and ground black pepper
salad leaves and (bell) pepper strips,
  to garnish

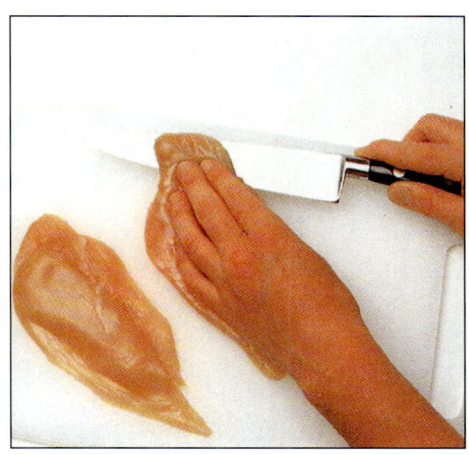

1. Slice each chicken breast portion in half horizontally, making two pieces of about the same thickness. Flatten them slightly with the heel of your hand.

2. Put the butter in a small pan and melt over a low heat. Do not let it brown.

Variation
For Cajun-spiced Fish, substitute six white fish fillets for the chicken. Do not slice the fish fillets in half, but season as for the chicken breast portions and cook for about 2 minutes on one side and 1½–2 minutes on the other, until the fish flakes easily when tested with the tip of a sharp knife.

3. Mix the remaining ingredients in a bowl, adding 7.5ml/1½ tsp each of salt and pepper. Brush the chicken on both sides with a little of the melted butter. Sprinkle evenly with the seasoning mixture.

4. Heat a large, heavy frying pan over a high heat for about 5–8 minutes, until a drop of water sprinkled on the surface sizzles.

5. Drizzle 5ml/1 tsp melted butter on to each chicken piece. Place them in the frying pan in an even layer, two or three at a time, and cook for 2–3 minutes, until the undersides begin to blacken. Turn the chicken over and cook the other side for 2–3 minutes more. Remove from the pan and keep hot while cooking successive batches. Serve hot with salad leaves and pepper strips.

Warm Chicken and Vegetable Salad

Succulent chicken is combined with vegetables in a light chilli dressing.

Preparation time 7 minutes
Cooking time 10 minutes

SERVES 6
50g/2oz mixed salad leaves
50g/2oz baby spinach leaves
50g/2oz watercress
30ml/2 tbsp chilli sauce
30ml/2 tbsp dry sherry
15ml/1 tbsp light soy sauce
15ml/1 tbsp tomato ketchup
10ml/2 tsp olive oil
8 shallots, finely chopped
1 garlic clove, crushed
350g/12oz skinless, boneless chicken breast portions, cut into thin strips
1 red (bell) pepper, seeded and sliced
175g/6oz/1½ cups mangetouts (snow peas)
400g/14oz can baby corn, drained and halved
275g/10oz can brown rice
salt and ground black pepper
fresh parsley sprig, to garnish

1. Tear any large salad leaves into smaller pieces. Arrange, with the spinach leaves, on a serving dish. Add the watercress and toss to mix.

2. In a small bowl, mix together the chilli sauce, dry sherry, light soy sauce and tomato ketchup and set aside.

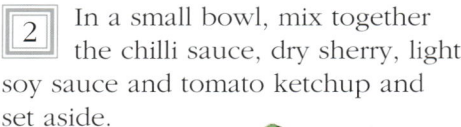

3. Heat the oil in a large non-stick frying pan or wok. Add the shallots and garlic and stir-fry over a medium heat for 1 minute.

4. Add the chicken and stir-fry for 3–4 minutes, then add the red pepper, mangetouts, baby corn and rice and stir-fry for 2–3 minutes more.

5. Pour in the chilli sauce mixture and stir-fry for 2–3 minutes, until hot and bubbling. Season to taste. Spoon the chicken mixture over the salad leaves, toss together to mix and serve immediately, garnished with fresh parsley.

COOK'S TIPS
Use other lean meat, such as turkey breast portions, beef or pork, in place of the chicken. You could also use prawns (shrimp). If using cooked prawns, add them to the pan with the chilli sauce so they are not overcooked.

Turkey with Yellow Pepper Sauce

Preparation time 6–8 minutes
Cooking time 12 minutes

Serves 4

30ml/2 tbsp olive oil
2 large yellow (bell) peppers, seeded and chopped
1 small onion, chopped
15ml/1 tbsp freshly squeezed orange juice
300ml/½ pint/1¼ cups chicken stock
4 turkey escalopes (US scallops)
75g/3oz/⅓ cup garlic-flavoured cream cheese
16 fresh basil leaves
25g/1oz/2 tbsp butter
salt and ground black pepper

1 To make the sauce, heat half the oil in a pan and gently cook the peppers and onion until beginning to soften. Add the orange juice and stock and cook until very soft. Meanwhile, lay the turkey escalopes between sheets of clear film (plastic wrap) and beat lightly.

2 Spread the turkey escalopes with the cream cheese. Chop half the basil and sprinkle on top, then roll up, tucking in the ends like an envelope. Secure with half a cocktail stick (toothpick).

3 Heat the remaining oil and the butter in a frying pan and cook the escalopes for 7–8 minutes, turning them frequently, until golden and cooked.

4 While the escalopes are cooking, press the pepper mixture through a sieve, or blend until smooth, then strain back into the pan. Season to taste and warm through, or serve cold, with the escalopes, garnished with the remaining basil leaves.

Cook's Tip
You could also use skinless, boneless chicken breast portions or veal escalopes (US scallops) in this dish.

COD WITH CAPER SAUCE

The quick and easy sauce with a slightly sharp and nutty flavour is a very effective way of enhancing this simple fish.

Preparation time 2 minutes
Cooking time 10 minutes

SERVES 4
4 cod steaks, about 175g/6oz each
115g/4oz/½ cup butter
15ml/1 tbsp small capers, rinsed, plus 15ml/1 tbsp vinegar from the caper jar
15ml/1 tbsp chopped fresh parsley
salt and ground black pepper
fresh tarragon sprigs, to garnish

[1] Preheat the grill (broiler). Season the cod. Melt 25g/1oz/ 2 tbsp of the butter, then brush some over one side of each piece of cod.

[2] Grill (broil) the cod for 4 minutes, turn the fish over, then brush with melted butter and cook for a further 4–5 minutes, or until the fish flakes easily.

[3] Meanwhile, heat the remaining butter until it turns golden brown, then add the vinegar followed by the capers and stir well.

[4] Pour the vinegar, butter and capers over the fish, sprinkle with parsley and garnish with the tarragon sprigs.

VARIATIONS
Thick tail fillets of cod or haddock could be used in place of the cod steaks. The sauce is also excellent with skate that has been pan-fried in butter.

Tagliatelle with Saffron Mussels

Preparation time 6 minutes
Cooking time 14 minutes

SERVES 4

1.75 kg/4–4½lb live mussels
150ml/¼ pint/ ⅔ cup dry white wine
2 shallots, chopped
350g/12oz fresh or dried tagliatelle
25g/1oz/2 tbsp butter
2 garlic cloves, crushed
250ml/8fl oz/1 cup double (heavy) cream
generous pinch of saffron threads
1 egg yolk
salt and ground black pepper
30ml/2 tbsp chopped fresh parsley, to garnish

1 Scrub the mussels well under cold running water. Remove the beards and discard any mussels that are damaged or that do not close immediately when tapped.

2 Place the mussels in a large pan with the wine and shallots. Cover and cook over a high heat, shaking occasionally, for 5–8 minutes, until the mussels have opened. Drain the mussels, reserving the liquid. Discard any mussels that remain closed. Shell most of the mussels and keep warm.

3 Bring the reserved cooking liquid to the boil, then reduce by half. Strain into a jug (pitcher).

4 Cook the tagliatelle in a large pan of lightly salted, boiling water until just tender. Meanwhile, melt the butter in a separate pan and cook the garlic for about a minute. Pour in the reserved mussel liquid, cream and saffron threads. Heat gently until the sauce thickens slightly. Remove the pan from the heat and stir in the egg yolk, shelled mussels and seasoning to taste.

5 Drain the tagliatelle, transfer to warmed serving bowls, then spoon the sauce over and sprinkle with chopped parsley. Garnish with the mussels in shells and serve.

COD CREOLE

Preparation time 5 minutes
Cooking time 10 minutes

SERVES 4

450g/1lb cod fillets, skinned
15ml/1 tbsp lime or lemon juice
10ml/2 tsp olive oil
1 medium onion, finely chopped
1 green (bell) pepper, seeded
   and sliced
2.5ml/ ½ tsp cayenne pepper
2.5ml/ ½ tsp garlic salt
400g/14oz can chopped tomatoes

COOK'S TIP
Be careful not to overcook the fish – or to let it bubble too vigorously in the sauce – or the chunks will break up. Test the fish frequently, and remove it from the heat the moment it is cooked.

[1] Cut the cod fillets into bitesize chunks and sprinkle with the lime or lemon juice.

[2] In a large pan, heat the olive oil and cook the onion and green pepper over a low heat until softened. Add the cayenne pepper and garlic salt.

[3] Stir in the cod chunks with the chopped tomatoes. Bring to a boil, then cover and simmer for about 5 minutes, or until the fish flakes easily when tested with the tip of a sharp knife. Serve with boiled rice or potatoes.

FIVE-SPICE FISH

Chinese mixtures of spicy, sweet and sour flavours are great with fish.

Preparation time 8 minutes
Cooking time 6 minutes

SERVES 4

4 white fish fillets, such as cod,
   haddock, whiting or hoki, about
   175g/6oz each
5ml/1 tsp Chinese five-spice powder
20ml/4 tsp cornflour (cornstarch)
15ml/1 tbsp sunflower oil
3 spring onions (scallions), shredded
5ml/1 tsp grated fresh root ginger
150g/5oz/2 cups button (white)
   mushrooms, sliced
115g/4oz/⅔ cup baby corn, sliced
30ml/2 tbsp soy sauce
45ml/3 tbsp dry sherry
5ml/1 tsp granulated sugar
salt and ground black pepper

[1] Toss the fish in the five-spice powder and cornflour to coat.

[2] Heat the oil in a frying pan or wok and stir-fry the spring onions, ginger, mushrooms and corn for 1 minute. Add the spiced fish and cook for 2 minutes, turning once.

[3] Mix together the soy sauce, sherry and sugar, then pour over the fish. Simmer for 2 minutes. Season to taste. Serve with noodles and stir-fried vegetables.

COOK'S TIP
Chinese noodles are available in most large supermarkets and make a very speedy accompaniment since they only need to be soaked in boiling water for a few minutes before being drained and served.

Fish Balls in Tomato Sauce

This quick meal is a good choice for young children, as you can be sure there are no bones.

Preparation time 4 minutes
Cooking time 14 minutes

SERVES 4

450g/1lb white fish fillets, such as haddock or cod, skinned
60ml/4 tbsp fresh wholemeal (wholewheat) breadcrumbs
30ml/2 tbsp chopped fresh chives
400g/14oz can chopped tomatoes
50g/2oz/½ cup button (white) mushrooms, sliced
salt and ground black pepper

1 Cut the fish fillets into large chunks and place in a food processor. Add the wholemeal breadcrumbs and chives. Season to taste with salt and pepper, and process until the fish is finely chopped, but still has some texture.

2 Divide the fish mixture into about 16 even-size pieces, then mould them into balls.

3 Place the tomatoes and mushrooms in a wide pan and cook over a medium heat until boiling. Add the fish balls, cover and simmer for about 10 minutes, until cooked. Serve hot.

Cook's Tips
Instead of using a can of chopped tomatoes and fresh mushrooms, you could substitute a jar of ready-made tomato and mushroom sauce. Just add the fish balls and simmer for about 10 minutes. When making this dish for young children, try cooking the fish balls in their favourite canned tomato soup – even children who turn up their noses at anything other than fish and chips (French fries) will love it.

Mackerel Kebabs with Parsley Dressing

Oily fish, such as mackerel, are ideal for grilling as they cook quickly and need no extra oil.

Preparation time 8 minutes
Cooking time 4 minutes

SERVES 4
450g/1lb mackerel fillets
finely grated rind and juice of 1 lemon
45ml/3 tbsp chopped fresh parsley
16 cherry tomatoes
8 pitted black olives
salt and ground black pepper

1 Cut the fish into 4cm/1½in chunks and toss in a bowl with half the lemon rind and juice, half the parsley and some seasoning.

2 Preheat the grill (broiler). Thread the chunks of fish on to eight long wooden or metal skewers, alternating them with the cherry tomatoes and olives. Grill (broil) the kebabs for 3–4 minutes, turning them occasionally, until the fish is cooked.

3 Mix the remaining lemon rind and juice with the remaining parsley in a small bowl, then season to taste with salt and pepper. Spoon this dressing over the kebabs and serve hot, with plain boiled rice or noodles and a leafy green salad.

Cook's Tip
When using wooden or bamboo kebab skewers, soak them in a bowl of cold water for 10 minutes to help prevent them from scorching.

Variations
Other firm-fleshed fish could be used in place of the mackerel – for a special occasion you could opt for salmon fillet or monkfish tail. Or try a mixture of the two, threading the fish chunks alternately on to the skewers with the tomatoes and olives.

Seafood Pilaff

This all-in-one-pan main course is a satisfying and surprisingly quick and easy meal for any day of the week. For a special meal, substitute dry white wine for the orange juice.

Preparation time 3 minutes
Cooking time 17 minutes

SERVES 4
10ml/2 tsp olive oil
250g/9oz/1¼ cups long grain rice
5ml/1 tsp ground turmeric
1 red (bell) pepper, seeded and diced
1 small onion, finely chopped
2 courgettes (zucchini), sliced
150g/5oz/2 cups button (white) mushrooms, halved
350ml/12fl oz/1½ cups fish or chicken stock
150ml/¼ pint/⅔ cup orange juice
350g/12oz white fish fillets, skinned and cubed
12 cooked, shelled mussels
salt and ground black pepper
grated rind of 1 orange, to garnish

1 Heat the oil in a large pan. Sauté the rice and ground turmeric over a low heat for about 1 minute.

2 Add the pepper, onion, courgettes and mushrooms. Stir in the stock and orange juice. Bring to the boil.

3 Reduce the heat and add the fish. Cover and simmer gently for about 15 minutes, until the rice is tender and the liquid absorbed. Stir in the mussels and heat thoroughly. Adjust the seasoning, sprinkle with orange rind and serve hot.

COOK'S TIP
If you prefer, use fresh mussels in the shell. Scrub well and discard any that remain open. Add to the pan 5 minutes before the end of cooking. Throw away any mussels that have not opened after cooking.

Salmon Pasta with Parsley Sauce

Preparation time 5 minutes
Cooking time 10–12 minutes

SERVES 4
450g/1lb salmon fillet, skinned
225g/8oz/2 cups dried pasta, such as penne or twists
175g/6oz cherry tomatoes, halved
150ml/¼ pint/⅔ cup low-fat crème fraîche
45ml/3 tbsp chopped fresh parsley
finely grated rind of ½ orange
salt and ground black pepper

COOK'S TIP
If you can't find low-fat crème fraîche, use ordinary crème fraîche or double (heavy) cream instead.

1 Cut the salmon into bitesize pieces, arrange on a heatproof plate and cover with foil.

2 Bring a large pan of salted water to the boil and add the pasta. Place the plate of salmon on top and cook for 10–12 minutes, until the pasta and salmon are cooked.

3 Drain the pasta and toss with the tomatoes and salmon. Mix together the crème fraîche, parsley, orange rind and pepper to taste, then toss with the salmon and pasta and serve hot or cold.

Warm Salmon Salad

Light and fresh, this salad should be served immediately, or you'll find the salad leaves will lose their bright colour and texture.

Preparation time 4–5 minutes
Cooking time 7 minutes

SERVES 4
450g/1lb salmon fillet, skinned
30ml/2 tbsp sesame oil
grated rind of ½ orange
juice of 1 orange
5ml/1 tsp Dijon mustard
15ml/1 tbsp chopped fresh tarragon
45ml/3 tbsp groundnut (peanut) oil
115g/4oz fine green beans, trimmed
175g/6oz mixed salad leaves, such as young spinach leaves, radicchio, frisée and oakleaf lettuce leaves
15ml/1 tbsp toasted sesame seeds

1. Cut the salmon into bitesize pieces, then make the dressing. Mix together the sesame oil, orange rind and juice, mustard, chopped tarragon and seasoning in a bowl.

2. Heat the groundnut oil in a frying pan. Add the salmon pieces and cook for 3–4 minutes, until golden but tender inside.

3. While the salmon is cooking, blanch the green beans in salted, boiling water for 5–6 minutes, until crisp-tender.

4. Add the dressing to the salmon. Toss gently over the heat for 30 seconds. Remove from the heat.

5. Arrange the salad leaves on serving plates. Drain the beans and arrange on top. Spoon over the salmon and cooking juices and serve, sprinkled with the sesame seeds.

SALMON WITH WATERCRESS SAUCE

Preparation time 2–3 minutes
Cooking time 16 minutes

SERVES 4
300ml/½pint/1¼ cups crème fraîche
30ml/2 tbsp chopped fresh tarragon
25g/1oz/2 tbsp unsalted (sweet) butter
15ml/1 tbsp sunflower oil
4 salmon fillets, skinned
1 garlic clove, crushed
120ml/4fl oz/½ cup dry white wine
1 bunch watercress
salt and ground black pepper

1 Gently heat the crème fraîche in a small pan until just beginning to boil. Remove the pan from the heat and stir in half the tarragon. Leave to infuse (steep) while you cook the fish.

2 Heat the butter and oil in a frying pan, add the salmon and cook for 3–5 minutes on each side. Remove from the pan and keep hot.

3 Add the garlic; cook briefly, then add the wine and cook until reduced to 15ml/1 tbsp.

4 Meanwhile, strip the leaves off the watercress stalks and chop finely. Discard any damaged leaves.

5 Strain the herb cream into the pan and cook for a few minutes, stirring until the sauce has thickened. Stir in the remaining tarragon and the watercress. Cook for a few minutes. Season, spoon over the salmon and serve.

Spanish-Style Hake

Cod and haddock steaks or cutlets will work just as well as hake.

Preparation time 3 minutes
Cooking time 15–16 minutes

SERVES 4

*30ml/2 tbsp olive oil
25g/1oz/2 tbsp butter
1 onion, chopped
3 garlic cloves, crushed
15ml/1 tbsp plain (all-purpose) flour
2.5ml/½ tsp paprika
4 hake cutlets, about 175g/6oz each
250g/8oz fine green beans, chopped
350ml/12fl oz/1½ cups fish stock
150ml/¼ pint/⅔ cup dry white wine
30ml/2 tbsp dry sherry
16–20 live mussels, cleaned
45ml/3 tbsp chopped fresh parsley
salt and ground black pepper
crusty bread, to serve*

1 Heat the oil and butter in a sauté or frying pan, add the onion and cook for 5 minutes, until softened, but not browned. Add the garlic and cook for 1 minute more.

2 Mix together the plain flour and paprika, then lightly dust over the hake cutlets. Push the onion and garlic to one side of the pan.

3 Add the hake cutlets to the pan and fry until golden on both sides. Stir in the beans, stock, wine, sherry and seasoning. Bring to the boil and cook for about 2 minutes.

4 Add the mussels and parsley, cover the pan and cook until the mussels have opened.

5 Discard any mussels that have not opened, then serve the hake in warmed soup bowls with crusty bread to mop up the juices.

SPAGHETTI WITH SEAFOOD SAUCE

Preparation time 4 minutes
Cooking time 16 minutes

SERVES 4

45ml/3 tbsp olive oil
1 medium onion, chopped
1 garlic clove, finely chopped
225g/8oz spaghetti
600ml/1 pint/2½ cups passata (bottled strained tomatoes)
15ml/1 tbsp tomato purée (paste)
5ml/1 tsp dried oregano
1 bay leaf
5ml/1 tsp granulated sugar
115g/4oz/1 cup cooked, peeled small shrimp, rinsed if canned
115g/4oz/1 cup cooked, peeled prawns (shrimp)
175g/6oz/1½ cups cooked clam or cockle meat, rinsed if canned
15ml/1 tbsp lemon juice
45ml/3 tbsp chopped fresh parsley
25g/1oz/2 tbsp butter
salt and ground black pepper
4 whole cooked prawns, to garnish

1   Heat the oil in a pan and add the onion and garlic. Cook over a medium heat for 5 minutes, until the onion has softened.

2   Meanwhile, cook the spaghetti in a large pan of salted, boiling water for 10–12 minutes. Stir the passata, tomato purée, oregano, bay leaf and sugar into the onion mixture and season well. Bring to the boil, then lower the heat and simmer for 2–3 minutes.

3   Add the shellfish, lemon juice and half the parsley. Stir, cover and cook for 6–7 minutes.

4   Drain the spaghetti when it is just tender; add the butter to the pan. Return the drained spaghetti to the pan and toss in the butter until well coated. Season well.

5   Divide the spaghetti among four warmed plates and top with the seafood sauce. Sprinkle with the remaining chopped parsley, garnish with the whole prawns and serve immediately.

PAN-FRIED PRAWNS IN THEIR SHELLS

Although expensive, this is a very quick and simple dish, ideal for an impromptu supper with friends. Serve with hot crusty Italian bread to scoop up the juices.

Preparation time 2–3 minutes
Cooking time 5–8 minutes

SERVES 4

60ml/4 tbsp extra virgin olive oil
32 large raw prawns (shrimp)
4 garlic cloves, finely chopped
120ml/4fl oz/½ cup Italian dry white vermouth
45ml/3 tbsp passata (bottled strained tomatoes)
salt and ground black pepper
chopped fresh flat leaf parsley, to garnish
crusty bread, to serve

1. Heat the olive oil in a large, heavy frying pan until just sizzling. Add the prawns and toss over a medium to high heat until their shells just begin to turn pink. Sprinkle the garlic over the prawns in the pan and toss again, then add the vermouth and let it bubble, tossing the prawns constantly so that they cook evenly and absorb the flavours of the garlic and vermouth.

2. Add the passata, with salt and pepper to taste. Stir until the prawns are thoroughly coated in the sauce. Serve immediately, sprinkled with the parsley and accompanied by plenty of hot crusty bread.

GRILLED RED MULLET WITH ROSEMARY

This recipe is very simple – the taste of grilled red mullet is so good in itself that it needs very little to bring out the flavour.

Preparation time 10 minutes
Cooking time 10 minutes

SERVES 4

4 red mullet or snapper, cleaned, about 275g/10oz each
4 garlic cloves, cut into thin slivers
75ml/5 tbsp olive oil
30ml/2 tbsp balsamic vinegar
10ml/2 tsp very finely chopped fresh rosemary
ground black pepper
coarse sea salt, to serve
fresh rosemary sprigs and lemon wedges, to garnish

1. Cut three diagonal slits in both sides of each fish. Push the garlic slivers into the slits. Place the fish in a single layer in a shallow dish. Whisk the oil, vinegar and rosemary in a bowl and add ground black pepper to taste.

VARIATION
Red mullet are extra delicious cooked on the barbecue. If possible, enclose them in a hinged wire basket so that they are easy to turn over.

2. Pour the vinaigrette mixture over the fish, cover with clear film (plastic wrap) and set aside for 8 minutes, or longer if you can spare the time. Lift the fish out of the dish and put it on a grill (broiler) rack. Reserve the marinade for basting.

3. Grill (broil) the fish for about 5 minutes on each side, turning once and brushing with the reserved marinade. Serve hot, sprinkled with sea salt and garnished with fresh rosemary sprigs and lemon wedges.

MACKEREL WITH MUSTARD AND LEMON

Mackerel must be really fresh to be enjoyed. Look for bright, firm-textured fish.

Preparation time 5 minutes
Cooking time 10–12 minutes

SERVES 4

4 fresh mackerel, about 275g/10oz each, gutted and cleaned
175–225g/6–8oz young spinach leaves

For the mustard and lemon butter
115g/4oz/½ cup butter, melted
30ml/2 tbsp wholegrain mustard
grated rind of 1 lemon
30ml/2 tbsp lemon juice
45ml/3 tbsp chopped fresh parsley
salt and ground black pepper

1. Cut off the mackerel heads just behind the gills, using a sharp knife, then slit the belly so that each fish can be opened out flat.

2. Place the fish skin-side up. With the heel of your hand, press along the backbone to loosen it.

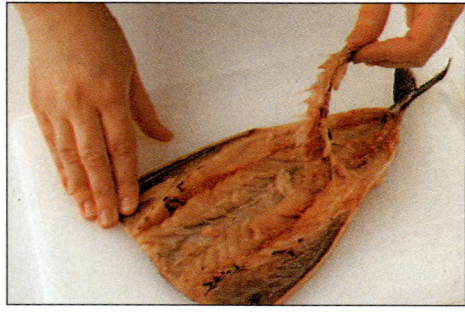

3. Turn the fish the right way up and pull the bone away. Cut off the tail and cut each fish in half lengthways. Wash and pat dry.

4. Score the skin three or four times, then season the fish. To make the mustard and lemon butter, mix together the melted butter, mustard, lemon rind and juice, parsley and seasoning. Place the mackerel on a grill (broiler) rack. Brush a little butter over the mackerel and grill (broil) for 5 minutes each side, basting occasionally.

5. Arrange the spinach leaves in the centre of four large plates. Place the mackerel on top. Heat the remaining flavoured butter in a small pan until sizzling and pour over the mackerel. Serve immediately.

Pan-steamed Mussels with Thai Herbs

Another simple and speedy dish. The lemon grass adds a refreshing tang.

Preparation time 5 minutes
Cooking time 5–7 minutes

SERVES 4–6

1kg/2¼ lb live mussels, cleaned
2 lemon grass stalks, finely chopped
4 shallots, chopped
4 kaffir lime leaves, coarsely torn
2 red chillies, sliced
15ml/1 tbsp Thai fish sauce
30ml/2 tbsp lime juice
chopped spring onions (scallions) and coriander (cilantro) leaves, to garnish

1 Place all the ingredients except the spring onions and coriander in a large pan. Stir well.

2 Cover the pan and place it over a medium-high heat. Steam for 5–7 minutes, shaking the pan occasionally, until the mussels open. Discard any mussels that do not open.

3 Lift out the cooked mussels with a slotted spoon and place on a serving dish.

4 Garnish the mussels with the chopped spring onions and coriander leaves. Serve immediately.

Chilli Prawns

This delightful, spicy combination makes a lovely light main course for a casual supper. Serve with rice, noodles or freshly cooked pasta and a leafy salad.

Preparation time 5 minutes
Cooking time 15 minutes

SERVES 3–4
45ml/3 tbsp olive oil
2 shallots, chopped
2 garlic cloves, chopped
1 red chilli, chopped
450g/1lb ripe tomatoes, peeled, seeded and chopped
15ml/1 tbsp tomato purée (paste)
1 bay leaf
1 fresh thyme sprig
90ml/6 tbsp dry white wine
450g/1lb cooked, peeled large prawns (shrimp)
salt and ground black pepper
coarsely torn basil leaves, to garnish

1. Heat the oil in a pan, then add the shallots, garlic and chilli. Cook until the garlic starts to brown.

2. Add the tomatoes, tomato purée, bay leaf, thyme, wine and seasoning. Bring to the boil, then reduce the heat and cook gently for about 10 minutes, stirring the sauce occasionally, until thickened. Remove and discard the herbs.

3. Stir the prawns into the sauce and heat through for a few minutes. Taste and adjust the seasoning. Sprinkle over the basil leaves and serve immediately.

COOK'S TIP
For a milder flavour, remove all the seeds from the chilli.

Scallops with Ginger

Scallops need little cooking, so are ideal for spontaneous suppers.

Preparation time 6 minutes
Cooking time 6–7 minutes

SERVES 4
8–12 shelled scallops
40g/1½oz/3 tbsp butter
2.5cm/1in piece of fresh root ginger, finely chopped
1 bunch spring onions (scallions), diagonally sliced
60ml/4 tbsp white vermouth
250ml/8fl oz/1 cup crème fraîche
salt and ground black pepper
chopped fresh parsley, to garnish

1. Remove the tough muscle opposite the coral on each scallop. Separate the coral and cut the white part of the scallop in half horizontally.

2. Melt the butter in a frying pan. Add the scallops, including the corals, if you like, and sauté for about 2 minutes until lightly browned. Take care not to overcook the scallops as this will toughen them. Lift out the scallops with a slotted spoon and transfer to a warmed serving dish. Keep hot.

3. Add the ginger and spring onions to the pan and stir-fry for 2 minutes. Pour in the vermouth and bubble until it has almost evaporated. Stir in the crème fraîche and cook for a few minutes until thickened. Season to taste.

4. Pour the sauce over the scallops, garnish and serve.

THAI PRAWN SALAD

This salad has the marvellous aromatic flavour of lemon grass.

Preparation time 17 minutes
Cooking time Nil

SERVES 4

250g/9oz cooked, peeled extra large tiger prawns (jumbo shrimp)
15ml/1 tbsp Thai fish sauce
30ml/2 tbsp lime juice
7.5ml/1½ tsp soft light brown sugar
1 small red chilli, finely chopped
1 spring onion (scallion), chopped
1 small garlic clove, crushed
2.5cm/1in piece of fresh lemon grass, finely chopped
30ml/2 tbsp chopped fresh coriander (cilantro)
45ml/3 tbsp dry white wine
8–12 small lettuce leaves, to serve
fresh coriander sprigs, to garnish

1. Place the tiger prawns in a bowl and add all the remaining ingredients except the lettuce. Stir well, cover and set aside for about 15 minutes, mixing and turning the prawns occasionally.

2. Arrange two or three of the lettuce leaves on each of four individual serving plates.

3. Spoon the prawn salad into the lettuce leaves. Garnish with coriander and serve immediately.

COOK'S TIP
If you can obtain raw prawns (shrimp), cook them in boiling water until pink and use instead of the cooked prawns.

CAJUN-SPICED FISH

Cajun food is becoming increasingly popular, and no wonder, as dishes like this one cook quickly and taste absolutely superb.

Preparation time 2–3 minutes
Cooking time 10–13 minutes

SERVES 4

5ml/1 tsp dried thyme
5ml/1 tsp dried oregano
5ml/1 tsp ground black pepper
1.5ml/¼ tsp cayenne pepper
10ml/2 tsp paprika
2.5ml/½ tsp garlic salt
4 tail end pieces of cod fillet (about 175g/6oz each)
75g/3oz/⅓ cup butter
½ red (bell) pepper, seeded and sliced
½ green (bell) pepper, seeded and sliced
fresh thyme, to garnish
grilled broiled tomatoes and sweet potato purée, to serve (optional)

1. Place all the herbs and spices in a large bowl and mix well. Lightly coat the fish fillets in the spice mixture.

2. Heat 25g/1oz/2 tbsp of the butter in a frying pan and gently cook the peppers for 5 minutes. Remove the peppers and keep hot.

3. Add the remaining butter to the pan and heat until sizzling. Add the cod fillets. Cook over a medium heat for 3–4 minutes on each side, until browned and cooked.

4. Transfer the fish to a warmed serving dish, surround with the peppers and garnish with thyme. Serve the spiced fish with some grilled (broiled) tomatoes and sweet potato purée, if you like.

COOK'S TIP
This blend of herbs and spices can be used to flavour any fish steaks or fillets and could also be used to jazz up pan-fried prawns (shrimp).

QUICK PITTA PIZZAS

Pitta breads make very good bases for quick thin and crispy pizzas, and they are easy to eat with your hands too. The perfect speedy snack.

Preparation time 5 minutes
Cooking time 8–10 minutes

SERVES 4
4 pitta breads
200ml/7fl oz jar pasta sauce
225g/8oz mozzarella cheese, sliced or grated
dried oregano or thyme, to sprinkle
salt and ground black pepper

Extra toppings – choose from
1 small red onion, thinly sliced and lightly cooked
75g/3oz/1¼ cup button (white) mushrooms, sliced and cooked
200g/7oz can corn, drained
2 jalapeño chillies, sliced
black or green olives, pitted and sliced
capers, drained

1. Prepare two or three toppings of your choice for the pizzas.

2. Preheat the grill (broiler) and lightly toast the pitta breads on both sides until golden.

COOK'S TIP
Teenagers love pitta pizzas, especially if they can assemble their own toppings. Strips of fried bacon and sliced pepperoni are great for non-vegetarians.

3. Spread pasta sauce on each pitta, right to the edge. This prevents the edges of the pitta from burning when they are returned to the grill.

4. Arrange cheese slices or grated cheese on top of each pitta and sprinkle with dried oregano or thyme. Add salt and pepper to taste.

5. Add the toppings of your choice and then grill (broil) the pizzas for about 5–8 minutes until they are golden brown and bubbling. Serve the pitta pizzas immediately.

French Bread Pizzas with Artichokes

Crunchy French bread makes an ideal base for these quick pizzas.

Preparation time 4 minutes
Cooking time 14–16 minutes

SERVES 4

15ml/1 tbsp sunflower oil
1 onion, chopped
1 green (bell) pepper, seeded
 and chopped
200g/7oz can chopped tomatoes
15ml/1 tbsp tomato purée (paste)
½ French stick
400g/14oz can artichoke hearts
115g/4oz mozzarella cheese, sliced
15ml/1 tbsp poppy seeds
salt and ground black pepper

1 Heat the oil in a frying pan. Add the chopped onion and pepper and cook for 4 minutes, until just softened.

2 Stir in the chopped tomatoes and the tomato purée. Cook for 4 minutes, stirring occasionally, then remove from the heat and add salt and pepper to taste.

3 Cut the piece of French stick in half lengthways. Cut each half in four to give eight pieces in all.

4 Spoon a little of the pepper and tomato mixture over each piece of bread. Preheat the grill (broiler).

5 Drain and slice the artichoke hearts. Arrange them on top of the pepper and tomato mixture. Cover with the mozzarella slices and sprinkle with the poppy seeds.

6 Arrange the French bread pizzas on a rack over a grill pan and grill (broil) for 6–8 minutes, until the cheese melts and is beginning to brown, then serve.

Brioche with Mixed Mushrooms

Mushrooms, served on toasted brioche, make a delectable lunch.

Preparation time 3–4 minutes
Cooking time 15 minutes

SERVES 4

75g/3oz/⅓ cup butter
1 vegetable stock (bouillon) cube
450g/1lb/scant 6½ cups shiitake
  mushrooms, caps only, sliced
225g/8oz/2 cups button (white)
  mushrooms, sliced
45ml/3 tbsp dry sherry
250ml/8fl oz/1 cup crème fraîche
10ml/2 tsp lemon juice
8 thick slices of brioche
salt and ground black pepper
fresh thyme, to garnish (optional)

1 Melt the butter in a large pan. Crumble in the stock cube and stir for about 30 seconds.

COOK'S TIP
If shiitake are not available, substitute more button (white) mushrooms.

2 Add the shiitake and button mushrooms to the pan and cook for 5 minutes over a medium to high heat, stirring occasionally.

3 Stir in the dry sherry. Cook for 1 minute, then add the crème fraîche. Cook, stirring, over a gentle heat for 5 minutes. Stir in the lemon juice and add salt and pepper to taste. Preheat the grill (broiler).

4 Toast the brioche slices under the grill until just golden on both sides. Spoon the mushrooms on top, flash briefly under the grill, and serve. Fresh thyme can be used as a garnish, if you like.

Mixed Pepper Pipérade

Preparation time 3–4 minutes
Cooking time 15 minutes

SERVES 4
30ml/2 tbsp olive oil
1 onion, chopped
1 red (bell) pepper
1 green (bell) pepper
4 tomatoes, peeled and chopped
1 garlic clove, crushed
4 large (US extra large) eggs
ground black pepper
toast, to serve

1 Heat the oil in a large frying pan and cook the onion gently until it becomes softened.

2 Remove the seeds from the red and green peppers and slice the flesh thinly. Stir the pepper slices into the onion and cook together gently for 5 minutes. Add the tomatoes and garlic, season with black pepper and cook for a further 5 minutes, or until the mixture has thickened slightly. In a small bowl, beat the eggs with 15ml/1 tbsp water.

3 Pour the egg mixture over the vegetables in the frying pan and cook for 2–3 minutes, stirring occasionally, until the pipérade has thickened to the consistency of lightly scrambled eggs. Serve immediately with hot toast.

Cook's Tips
Choose eggs that have been date-stamped for freshness. Do not stir the pipérade too much or the eggs may become rubbery.

Broccoli and Cauliflower Gratin

Broccoli and cauliflower make an attractive combination.

Preparation time 3 minutes
Cooking time 11 minutes

SERVES 4
1 small cauliflower, about 250g/9oz
250g/9oz broccoli
150ml/¼ pint/⅔ cup natural (plain) yogurt
115g/4oz/1 cup grated Cheddar cheese
5ml/1 tsp wholegrain mustard
30ml/2 tbsp wholemeal (whole-wheat) breadcrumbs
salt and ground black pepper

1. Break the cauliflower and broccoli into small florets, then cook in salted, boiling water for about 8 minutes, or until tender. Drain thoroughly, then transfer to a flameproof dish.

2. Mix the yogurt, cheese and mustard. Season with pepper and spoon over the cauliflower and broccoli. Preheat the grill (broiler).

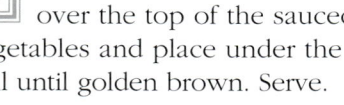

3. Sprinkle the breadcrumbs over the top of the sauced vegetables and place under the hot grill until golden brown. Serve.

COOK'S TIP
When preparing the cauliflower and broccoli, discard the tougher part of the stalk, then break the florets into even-size pieces, so that they cook evenly. Any tender pieces of stalk on the broccoli can be peeled, thinly sliced and cooked with the florets.

Cracked Wheat and Fennel Salad

Preparation time 18 minutes
Cooking time 2 minutes

Serves 4
115g/4oz/³⁄₄ cup cracked wheat
115g/4oz green beans, chopped
1 large fennel bulb, finely chopped
1 small orange, rind grated
1 garlic clove, crushed
30–45ml/2–3 tbsp sunflower oil
15ml/1 tbsp white wine vinegar
salt and ground black pepper
chopped red or orange (bell) pepper, to garnish

1 Place the cracked wheat in a bowl and cover with boiling water. Leave for 10 minutes. Drain well and squeeze out any excess water. Tip into a bowl.

2 Blanch the green beans in boiling water for 2 minutes. Drain. Stir into the drained wheat with the fennel. Peel and segment the orange and stir into the salad.

3 Add the garlic to the orange rind, then add the oil, wine vinegar and seasoning to taste, and mix thoroughly. Pour this dressing over the salad, mix well. If time permits, chill the salad for 1–2 hours.

4 Serve the salad sprinkled with the red or orange pepper.

RUNNER BEANS WITH TOMATOES

Young runner beans should not have "strings" down the sides, but older ones will, and the strings should be removed before cooking.

Preparation time 2 minutes
Cooking time 13–18 minutes

SERVES 4
*675g/1½lb runner (green)
  beans, sliced
40g/1½oz/3 tbsp butter
4 ripe tomatoes, peeled and chopped
salt and ground black pepper
chopped fresh tarragon, to garnish*

COOK'S TIP
Other green beans can be used instead of runner beans, but reduce the cooking time slightly.

[1] Add the beans to a pan of boiling water, return to the boil, then boil for 3 minutes. Drain well.

[2] Heat the butter in a pan and add the tomatoes, beans and seasoning. Cover the pan and simmer gently for 10–15 minutes, until the beans are tender.

[3] Tip the beans and tomatoes into a warm serving dish and sprinkle over the chopped tarragon. Serve hot as an accompaniment.

SPINACH AND BEETROOT SALAD

Preparation time 5 minutes
Cooking time 1 minute

SERVES 4–6
*200g/7oz young spinach leaves
45ml/3 tbsp light olive oil
5ml/1 tsp caraway seeds
juice of 1 orange
5ml/1 tsp caster (superfine) sugar
675g/1½lb cooked beetroot (beet)
salt and ground black pepper
chopped fresh parsley, to garnish*

[1] Arrange the spinach leaves in a shallow salad bowl.

[2] Heat the oil in a pan. Add the caraway seeds, orange juice and sugar. Shake over the heat to warm through.

[3] Dice and add the beetroot and shake the pan to coat.

[4] Spoon the warm beetroot and dressing mixture over the spinach leaves and sprinkle with the chopped parsley. Serve the salad immediately either as a main course or as an accompaniment.

COOK'S TIP
Use freshly cooked beetroot, not those that have been steeped in vinegar.

VEGETABLE AND SATAY SALAD

To cook this tasty salad in the allotted time, you will need to cook the potatoes and the other vegetables simultaneously.

Preparation time 5 minutes
Cooking time 12–14 minutes

SERVES 4

450g/1lb baby new potatoes
1 small head cauliflower, broken into small florets
225g/8oz green beans, trimmed
400g/14oz can chickpeas, drained
115g/4oz/2 cups watercress sprigs
115g/4oz/2 cups beansprouts
8 spring onions (scallions), sliced
60ml/4 tbsp crunchy peanut butter
150ml/¼ pint/⅔ cup hot water
5ml/1 tsp chilli sauce
10ml/2 tsp soft brown sugar
5ml/1 tsp soy sauce
5ml/1 tsp lime juice

1 Put the potatoes into a pan and add water to cover. Bring to the boil and cook for 10–12 minutes, or until the potatoes are just tender when pierced with the point of a sharp knife. Drain and refresh under cold running water. Drain the potatoes again.

2 Meanwhile, bring another pan of salted water to the boil. Add the cauliflower and cook for about 5 minutes, then add the beans and cook for 5 minutes more. Drain both vegetables, refresh under cold water and drain again.

3 Put the cauliflower and beans into a large bowl and add the chickpeas. Halve the potatoes and add. Toss lightly. Mix the watercress, beansprouts and spring onions. Divide among four plates and pile the cooked vegetables on top.

4 Put the peanut butter into a bowl and stir in the water. Add the chilli sauce, brown sugar, soy sauce and lime juice. Whisk well then drizzle the dressing over the salad. Serve immediately, with lime wedges, if you like.

Courgette Puffs with Mixed Leaf Salad

This unusual salad consists of deep-fried courgettes, flavoured with mint and served warm on a bed of salad leaves with a balsamic dressing.

Preparation time 5 minutes
Cooking time 6 minutes

SERVES 2–3

450g/1lb courgettes (zucchini)
75g/3oz/1½ cups fresh white breadcrumbs
1 egg
pinch of cayenne pepper
15ml/1 tbsp chopped fresh mint
oil, for deep frying
15ml/1 tbsp balsamic vinegar
45ml/3 tbsp extra virgin olive oil
200g/7oz mixed salad leaves
salt and ground black pepper

1 Trim the courgettes. Coarsely grate them and put into a colander. Squeeze out the excess water, then put the courgettes into a large bowl.

2 Add the white breadcrumbs, egg, cayenne pepper and chopped fresh mint, with salt and pepper to taste. Mix well, with a spoon or clean hands.

3 Shape the courgette and breadcrumb mixture into balls, about the size of walnuts.

4 Heat the oil for deep-frying to 180°C/350°F, or until a cube of bread, when added to the oil, browns in 30–40 seconds. Deep-fry the courgette balls, in batches, for 2 minutes. Drain on kitchen paper.

5 Whisk the vinegar and oil together and season well.

6 Put the salad leaves in a bowl and pour over the dressing. Toss lightly to coat the leaves evenly. Add the courgette puffs and toss lightly together. Serve immediately, while the courgette puffs are still hot and crisp.

Herb Omelette with Tomato Salad

This is ideal as a snack or a light lunch – use flavourful, fresh plum tomatoes in season.

Preparation time 6 minutes
Cooking time 6 minutes

SERVES 4
4 eggs, beaten
30ml/2 tbsp chopped, mixed fresh herbs
knob (pat) of butter
45–60ml/3–4 tbsp olive oil
15ml/1 tbsp fresh orange juice
5ml/1 tsp red wine vinegar
5ml/1 tsp wholegrain mustard
2 large beef tomatoes, thinly sliced
salt and ground black pepper
fresh herb sprigs, to garnish

1. Beat the eggs, herbs and seasoning together. Heat the butter and a little of the oil in an omelette pan.

2. When the fats are just sizzling, pour in the egg mixture and leave to set for about 5 minutes until almost cooked through, stirring very occasionally with a fork.

3. Meanwhile, heat the rest of the oil in a small pan with the orange juice, vinegar and mustard, and add salt and pepper to taste.

4. Roll up the cooked omelette and cut neatly into 1cm/½in wide strips. Keep them rolled up and transfer immediately to warmed plates.

5. Arrange the sliced tomatoes on the plates with the omelette rolls and pour on the warm dressing. Garnish with herb sprigs and serve.

Three-cheese Croûtes

Preparation time 2–3 minutes
Cooking time 10–15 minutes

SERVES 2–4
4 thick slices of slightly stale bread
a little butter or mustard
75g/3oz Brie cheese
45ml/3 tbsp fromage frais (farmer's cheese)
50g/2oz/½ cup grated Cheddar cheese
1 small garlic clove, crushed
salt and ground black pepper
black olives, to garnish

Cook's Tips
If you have Brie that will not ripen fully, this is an excellent way of using it up. You'll need a knife and fork to eat this tasty appetizer. Instead of the simple black olive garnish, you could serve it with tangy whole-fruit cranberry sauce.

1. Preheat the oven to 200°C/400°F/Gas 6. Place the bread slices on a baking sheet and spread with either butter or mustard.

2. Cut the Brie into thin slices and arrange evenly on the bread.

3. Mix together the fromage frais, grated Cheddar cheese, garlic and seasoning to taste. Spread over the Brie and the bread, taking the mixture right to the corners.

4. Bake for 10–15 minutes, or until golden and bubbling. Serve immediately, garnished with black olives.

Lemon and Parmesan Capellini with Herb Bread

Cream with Parmesan is flavoured with lemon for a superb pasta sauce.

Preparation time 5 minutes
Cooking time 2–12 minutes

SERVES 2

½ Granary (multigrain) baguette
50g/2oz/¼ cup butter, softened
1 garlic clove, crushed
30ml/2 tbsp chopped fresh herbs
225g/8oz dried or fresh capellini
250ml/8fl oz/1 cup single (light) cream
75g/3oz/1 cup grated Parmesan cheese
finely grated rind of 1 lemon
salt and ground black pepper

1. Preheat the oven to 200°C/400°F/Gas 6. Cut the baguette into thick slices.

2. Put the butter in a bowl and beat with the garlic and herbs. Spread thickly over each slice of Granary bread.

3. Reassemble the baguette. The garlic herb butter will help to hold the slices together. Wrap in foil, support on a baking sheet and bake for 10 minutes.

4. Meanwhile, bring a large pan of water to the boil and cook the pasta until just tender. Dried pasta will take 10–12 minutes; fresh pasta will be ready in 2–3 minutes.

5. Pour the cream into another pan and bring to the boil. Stir in the grated Parmesan and lemon rind. The sauce should thicken in about 30 seconds.

6. Drain the pasta, return it to the pan and toss with the sauce. Season to taste with salt and pepper and sprinkle with a little chopped fresh parsley and more grated lemon rind, if you like. Serve with the hot herb bread.

Tagliatelle with Tomatoes and Black Olives

Sun-dried tomatoes add pungency to this dish, while the grilled fresh tomatoes give it some bite.

Preparation time 5 minutes
Cooking time 10–12 minutes

SERVES 4
*45ml/3 tbsp olive oil
1 garlic clove, crushed
1 small onion, chopped
60ml/4 tbsp dry white wine
6 sun-dried tomatoes, chopped
30ml/2 tbsp chopped fresh parsley
50g/2oz/ 1/2 cup pitted black
  olives, halved
450g/1lb fresh tagliatelle
4 tomatoes, halved
Parmesan cheese, to serve
salt and ground black pepper*

1. Heat 30ml/2 tbsp of the oil in a pan. Add the garlic and onion and cook for 2–3 minutes, stirring occasionally. Add the wine, sun-dried tomatoes and the parsley. Cook for 2 minutes. Stir in the black olives, lower the heat and leave the sauce over a low heat.

COOK'S TIP
It is essential to buy Parmesan in a piece for this dish. Find a good source – fresh Parmesan should not be unacceptably hard – and shave or grate it yourself. The flavour will be much more intense than that of the ready-grated product.

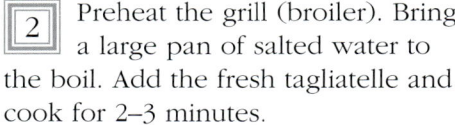

2. Preheat the grill (broiler). Bring a large pan of salted water to the boil. Add the fresh tagliatelle and cook for 2–3 minutes.

3. Put the tomatoes on a baking sheet, brush with the remaining oil and grill (broil) for 3–4 minutes.

4. When the pasta rises to the surface of the boiling water, it is ready. Drain it thoroughly, return it to the pan and toss with the sauce. Pile into a bowl and add the grilled tomatoes. Grind black pepper over the top and add Parmesan shavings.

Pasta with Broccoli and Artichokes

Preparation time 5 minutes
Cooking time 13 minutes

SERVES 4

105ml/7 tbsp olive oil
1 red (bell) pepper, quartered, seeded, and thinly sliced
1 onion, halved and thinly sliced
5ml/1 tsp dried thyme
45ml/3 tbsp sherry vinegar
450g/1lb fresh or dried pasta shapes, such as penne or fusilli
2 x 175g/6oz jars marinated artichoke hearts, drained and thinly sliced
150g/5oz cooked broccoli, chopped
20–25 black olives, pitted and chopped
30ml/2 tbsp chopped fresh parsley
salt and ground black pepper

1. Heat 30ml/2 tbsp of the olive oil in a non-stick frying pan. Add the red pepper and onion and cook over a low heat, stirring occasionally, for 8–10 minutes, or until the vegetables are just soft.

2. Stir in the thyme and sherry vinegar. Cook for 30 seconds more, stirring, then set aside.

3. Meanwhile, cook the pasta in a large pan of salted, boiling water until just tender (10–12 minutes for dried; 2–3 minutes for fresh). Drain, then transfer to a serving large bowl. Add 30ml/2 tbsp of the oil and toss well to coat.

4. Add the artichokes, broccoli, olives, parsley, onion mixture and remaining oil to the pasta. Season with salt and pepper. Toss to blend. Leave to stand for 5 minutes before serving, longer if time permits.

Pasta with Spring Vegetables

Preparation and cooking time 20 minutes

SERVES 4
115g/4oz/1 cup broccoli florets
115g/4oz baby leeks
225g/8oz asparagus, trimmed
1 small fennel bulb
115g/4oz/1 cup fresh or frozen peas
40g/1½oz/3 tbsp butter
1 shallot, chopped
45ml/3 tbsp chopped fresh mixed herbs, such as parsley, thyme and sage
300ml/½ pint/1¼ cups double (heavy) cream
350g/12oz dried penne pasta
salt and ground black pepper
freshly grated Parmesan cheese, to serve

1. Divide the broccoli into sprigs. Cut the leeks and asparagus diagonally into 5cm/2in lengths. Trim the fennel bulb and cut into wedges.

2. Cook the vegetables in salted, boiling water until just tender. Remove with a slotted spoon and keep hot.

3. Melt the butter in a separate pan, add the chopped shallot and cook, stirring occasionally, until softened, but not browned. Stir in the herbs and cream and cook for a few minutes, until slightly thickened.

4. Meanwhile, cook the pasta in salted, boiling water until just tender. Drain well and add to the sauce with the vegetables. Toss gently and season with black pepper.

5. Serve the pasta immediately with a generous sprinkling of freshly grated Parmesan.

RED FRIED RICE

This vibrant rice dish owes its appeal as much to the bright colours of red onion, red pepper and cherry tomatoes as it does to their flavours.

Preparation time 3–4 minutes
Cooking time 13–15 minutes

SERVES 2

225g/8oz/generous 1 cup basmati rice
30ml/2 tbsp groundnut (peanut) oil
1 large red onion, chopped
1 red (bell) pepper, seeded and chopped
350g/12oz cherry tomatoes, halved
4 eggs, beaten
salt and ground black pepper

1. Wash the rice several times in a bowl of cold water. Drain well. Bring a large pan of water to the boil, add the rice and cook for 10–12 minutes.

2. Meanwhile, heat the oil in a wok until very hot. Add the onion and red pepper and stir-fry for 2–3 minutes. Add the cherry tomatoes and stir-fry for a further 2 minutes.

3. Pour in the beaten eggs all at once. Cook for 30 seconds without stirring, then stir to break up the eggs as they set.

4. Drain the cooked rice well, add to the wok and toss it over the heat with the egg and vegetable mixture for 3 minutes. Season to taste with salt and pepper.

KEDGEREE WITH GREEN BEANS AND MUSHROOMS

Crunchy, cooked green beans and brown cap mushrooms are the star ingredients in this vegetarian version of an old favourite.

Preparation time 3–4 minutes
Cooking time 16 minutes

SERVES 2–3
115g/4oz/scant ⅔ cup basmati rice
3 eggs
175g/6oz green beans, trimmed
50g/2oz/¼ cup butter
1 onion, finely chopped
225g/8oz/2 cups brown cap (cremini) mushrooms, quartered
30ml/2 tbsp single (light) cream
15ml/1 tbsp chopped fresh parsley
salt and ground black pepper

1. Wash the rice several times in a bowl of cold water. Drain thoroughly. Bring a pan of water to the boil, add the rice and cook for 10–12 minutes, until the grains are just tender.

2. Meanwhile, half-fill a second pan with water, add the eggs and bring to the boil. Lower the heat and simmer for 8 minutes. Drain the eggs, cool them under cold water, then remove the shells.

3. Bring another pan of water to the boil and cook the green beans for 5 minutes. Drain, refresh under cold running water, then drain again.

4. Melt the butter in a large frying pan. Add the onion and mushrooms. Cook for 2–3 minutes over a moderate heat.

VARIATION
Omit the beans and cook two sliced celery sticks with the onion and mushrooms. Garnish with toasted almonds.

5. Drain the rice well and add it to the onion mixture with the beans. Stir lightly. Cook for about 2 minutes. Cut the hard-boiled eggs in wedges and add them to the pan.

6. Stir in the cream and parsley, taking care not to break up the eggs. Reheat the kedgeree, but do not allow it to boil, then serve.

Red Fruit Filo Baskets

Filo pastry is light as air and makes a very elegant dessert.

Preparation time 8 minutes
Cooking time 6–8 minutes

SERVES 6

3 sheets filo pastry (about 90g/3½oz)
15ml/1 tbsp sunflower oil
175g/6oz/1½ cups soft fruits, such as redcurrants, strawberries and raspberries
250ml/8fl oz/1 cup Greek yogurt
5ml/1 tsp icing sugar

1. Preheat the oven to 200°C/400°F/Gas 6. Cut the sheets of filo pastry into 18 squares with sides about 10cm/4in long. Cover the filo with clear film to stop it from drying out.

2. Brush each filo square very thinly with oil, and then arrange the squares overlapping in six small patty tins, layering them in threes. Bake for 6–8 minutes, until crisp and golden. Lift the baskets out carefully and leave them to cool for 5–10 minutes on a wire rack.

3. Reserve a few sprigs of redcurrants on their stems for decoration and string the rest. Stir into the yogurt with the strawberries and raspberries.

4. Spoon the yogurt mixture into the filo baskets. Decorate them with the reserved sprigs of redcurrants and sprinkle them with icing sugar to serve.

VARIATIONS
Other soft fruits can be used instead of redcurrants, strawberries and raspberries. Try blueberries or blackberries for a change, or use sliced bananas, nectarines, peaches or kiwi fruit.

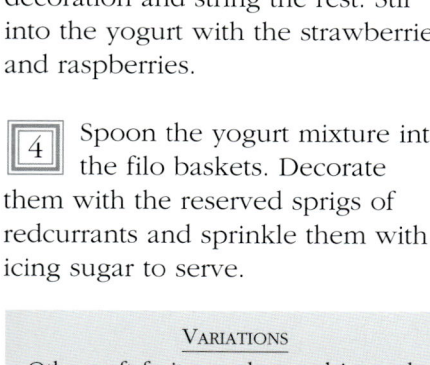

Apple Soufflé Omelette

Slightly caramelized apples make a delicious autumn filling.

Preparation time 3–4 minutes
Cooking time 8 minutes

SERVES 2
4 eggs, separated
30ml/2 tbsp single (light) cream
15ml/1 tbsp caster (superfine) sugar
15g/½oz/1 tbsp butter
icing (confectioners') sugar,
  for dredging
For the filling
1 eating apple, peeled, cored
  and sliced
25g/1oz/2 tbsp butter
30ml/2 tbsp soft light brown sugar
45ml/3 tbsp single (light) cream

1 To make the filling, sauté the apple slices in the butter and sugar until just tender. Stir in the cream and keep warm.

2 Beat the egg yolks with the cream and sugar. Whisk the egg whites until stiff, then fold into the yolks. Preheat the grill (broiler).

3 Melt the butter in a large, heavy frying pan, pour in the soufflé mixture and spread evenly. Cook until golden underneath, then brown the top under the grill.

4 Slide the omelette on to a plate, add the apple mixture, then fold over. Sift the icing sugar over thickly, then brand with a hot metal skewer. Serve immediately.

PINEAPPLE FLAMBÉ

Flambéing means adding alcohol and then burning it off so the flavour is not too overpowering.

Preparation time 5 minutes
Cooking time 1–2 minutes

SERVES 4
1 large, ripe pineapple
40g/1½oz/3 tbsp unsalted (sweet) butter
40g/1½oz/3 tbsp soft light brown sugar
60ml/4 tbsp fresh orange juice
30ml/2 tbsp brandy
25g/1oz/2 tbsp slivered almonds, toasted

1. Cut away the top and base of the pineapple. Then cut down the sides, removing all the dark "eyes", but leaving the pineapple in a good shape.

2. Cut the pineapple into thin slices and, with an apple corer, remove the hard central core.

3. In a large frying pan melt the butter with the sugar and orange juice. Add the pineapple slices and cook for about 1 minute, turning the slices once.

4. Add the brandy and light with a match immediately. Let the flames die down and then sprinkle with the almonds and serve with ice cream or thick yogurt.

WARM PEARS IN CIDER

Preparation and cooking time 20 minutes

SERVES 4
1 lemon
50g/2oz/¼ cup caster (superfine) sugar
a little grated nutmeg
250ml/8fl oz/1 cup sweet (hard) cider
4 firm, ripe pears

1. Carefully remove the rind from the lemon with a potato peeler.

2. Squeeze the juice from the lemon into a pan, add the rind, sugar, nutmeg and cider and heat to dissolve the sugar.

3. Carefully peel the pears, leaving the stalks on if possible, and place them in the pan of sweetened, spiced cider. Poach the pears over a medium heat for 10–15 minutes, until almost tender, turning them frequently.

4. Transfer the pears to individual serving dishes using a slotted spoon. Simmer the liquid over a high heat until it reduces slightly and becomes syrupy.

5. Pour the warm syrup over the pears, and serve immediately with freshly made custard, whipped cream or ice cream.

COOK'S TIP
To get pears of just the right firmness, you may have to buy them slightly under-ripe and then wait a day or more. Soft pears are no good at all for this dish.

Cool Green Fruit Salad

A sophisticated, simple fruit salad for any time of year.

Preparation time 20 minutes
Cooking time 30 seconds

SERVES 6
3 Ogen melons
115g/4oz/1 cup green seedless grapes
2 kiwi fruit
1 star fruit
1 green-skinned apple
1 lime
175ml/6fl oz/¾ cup sparkling white grape juice

1. Cut the melons in half and scoop out the seeds. Keeping the shells intact, scoop out the flesh with a melon baller, or scoop it out with a spoon and cut into bitesize cubes. Reserve the melon shells.

2. Remove any stems from the grapes, and, if they are large, cut them in half. Peel and chop the kiwi fruit. Thinly slice the star fruit. Core and thinly slice the apple and place the slices in a bowl, with the melon, grapes, kiwi fruit and star fruit. Mix gently.

3. Thinly pare the rind from the lime and cut it in fine strips. Blanch the strips in boiling water for 30 seconds and then drain them and rinse them in cold water. Squeeze the juice from the lime and toss it into the fruit.

4. Spoon the prepared fruit into the reserved melon shells. Chill the shells if you have time, or serve immediately, spooning the grape juice over the fruit and sprinkling it with the lime rind.

Cook's Tip
If you're serving this dessert on a hot summer day, serve the filled melon shells nestling on a platter of crushed ice to keep them beautifully cool.

PRUNE AND ORANGE POTS

A simple dessert, made in minutes. It can be served straight away, but is best chilled for about half an hour.

Preparation time 4 minutes
Cooking time 7 minutes

SERVES 4
225g/8oz/1 cup ready-to-eat prunes
150ml/¼ pint/⅔ cup fresh orange juice
250ml/8fl oz/1 cup natural (plain) yogurt
thin shreds of orange rind, to decorate

VARIATIONS
This dessert can also be made with other ready-to-eat dried fruit, such as apricots or peaches. Add a dash of brandy or Cointreau to the yogurt for a special occasion dessert.

1 Remove the stones (pits) from the prunes and coarsely chop them. Place them in a pan and pour in the orange juice.

3 Remove from the heat, leave to cool slightly and then beat well with a wooden spoon, until the fruit breaks down to a coarse purée.

5 Spoon the mixture into four stemmed glasses or individual dishes. Smooth the tops, but don't lose the swirled effect.

2 Bring the juice to the boil, stirring. Reduce the heat, cover and simmer for 5 minutes, until the prunes are tender and the liquid is reduced by half.

4 Transfer the mixture to a bowl. Stir in the yogurt, swirling the yogurt and fruit purée together lightly with a spoon to give an attractive marbled effect.

6 Blanch the shreds of orange rind in boiling water, drain and use a few shreds to decorate each dessert. Serve immediately or chill if time permits.

Orange Yogurt Brûlées

A luxurious treat, but one that is lower in fat than the classic brûlées.

Preparation time 6–8 minutes
Cooking time 3–4 minutes

SERVES 4

2 oranges
150ml/ ¼ pint/ ⅔ cup Greek (US strained plain) yogurt
60ml/4 tbsp crème fraîche
45ml/3 tbsp golden caster (superfine) sugar
30ml/2 tbsp light muscovado (brown) sugar

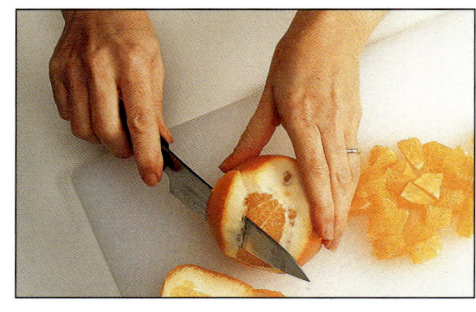

1 With a sharp knife, cut away all the peel and white pith from the oranges and chop the fruit. Or, if there's time, segment the oranges, removing all the membrane.

2 Place the fruit in the bases of four individual flameproof dishes. Mix together the yogurt and crème fraîche and spoon over the oranges. Preheat the grill (broiler).

3 Mix together the two sugars and sprinkle them thickly and evenly over the tops of the dishes.

4 Place the dishes under the grill, close to the heat, for 3–4 minutes, or until the sugar melts and turns a rich golden brown. Serve warm or cold.

Cook's Tip
For a lighter version, simply use 250ml/8fl oz/1 cup low-fat natural yogurt instead of Greek (US strained plain) yogurt and crème fraîche.

GRILLED NECTARINES WITH RICOTTA AND SPICE

This easy dessert is good at any time of year — use canned peach halves if fresh nectarines are not available.

Preparation time 3 minutes
Cooking time 6–8 minutes

SERVES 4
4 ripe nectarines
115g/4oz/½ cup ricotta cheese
15ml/1 tbsp light muscovado (brown) sugar
2.5ml/½ tsp ground star anise

1 Cut the nectarines in half and remove the stones (pits).

2 Arrange the nectarines, cut-side up, in a wide flameproof dish or on a baking sheet.

COOK'S TIP
Star anise has a warm, rich flavour – if you can't get it, try ground cloves or mixed (apple pie) spice instead.

3 Put the ricotta cheese in a bowl and stir in the sugar. Using a teaspoon, spoon the mixture into the hollow of each nectarine half. Preheat the grill (broiler).

4 Sprinkle with the star anise. Place under the grill and cook for 6–8 minutes, or until the nectarines are hot and bubbling. Serve warm.

INDEX

A
apples: apple soufflé omelette, 89
  smoked mackerel and apple dip, 26
artichokes: French bread pizzas with, 71
  pasta with broccoli and, 84
asparagus: asparagus rolls with herb
    butter sauce, 30
  with orange sauce, 29
avocado and papaya salad, 35

B
beef: beef strips with orange and ginger, 39
  chilli beef nachos, 24
  Stilton beefburgers, 37
beetroot: spinach and beetroot salad, 76
beets *see* beetroot
bell peppers *see* peppers
brioche with mixed mushrooms, 72
broccoli: broccoli and cauliflower gratin, 74
  haddock and broccoli chowder, 22
  pasta with artichokes and, 84

C
Cajun-spiced chicken, 47
Cajun-spiced fish, 68
Caribbean chicken kebabs, 46
cauliflower: broccoli and cauliflower
    gratin, 74
cheese: broccoli and cauliflower gratin, 74
  lemon and Parmesan capellini with herb
    bread, 82
  quick pitta pizzas, 70
  Stilton beefburgers, 37
  three-cheese croûtes, 80
  see also ricotta
chicken: Cajun-spiced, 47
  Caribbean chicken kebabs, 46
  chicken chow mein, 45
  warm chicken and vegetable salad, 48
chilli prawns, 66
chocolate sauce, 13
cod: Cajun-spiced fish, 68
  cod Creole, 52
  with caper sauce, 50
corn and crab chowder, 23
corned beef and egg hash, 36
courgette puffs with mixed leaf salad, 79
crab: corn and crab chowder, 23
  egg and tomato salad with, 32
cracked wheat and fennel salad, 75

D
dips, 26

E
eggs: baked eggs with tarragon, 27
  corned beef and egg hash, 36
  egg and tomato salad with crab, 32
  mixed pepper pipérade, 73
  poached eggs with spinach, 28

F
fennel: cracked wheat and fennel salad, 75
fish: fish balls in tomato sauce, 54
  five-spice fish, 52
  seafood pilaff, 56
five-spice fish, 52
French bread pizzas with artichokes, 71
fruit: red fruit filo baskets, 88
fruit salads: cool green, 92

G
garlic: Spanish garlic soup, 20
green beans: kedgeree with mushrooms
    and green beans, 87

H
hake, Spanish-style, 60
herb omelette with tomato salad, 80

K
kebabs: Caribbean chicken, 46
  mackerel with parsley dressing, 55
kedgeree with green beans and
  mushrooms, 87
kidneys: veal kidneys with mustard, 38

L
lamb chops with mint vinaigrette, 42
lemon and Parmesan capellini with
    herb bread, 82
liver: lamb's liver with peppers, 40

M
mackerel: kebabs with parsley dressing, 55
  with mustard and lemon, 64
  see also smoked mackerel
menus, 14–15
mushrooms: brioche with mixed
    mushrooms, 72
  kedgeree with green beans and, 87
mussels: pan-steamed mussels with Thai
    herbs, 65
  tagliatelle with saffron mussels, 51

N
nachos, chilli beef, 24
nectarines: grilled with ricotta and
    spice, 95
noodles: chicken chow mein, 45

O
omelettes: apple soufflé, 89
  herb with tomato salad, 80
orange: orange yogurt brûlées, 94
  prune and orange pots, 93

P
pancakes, 13
papaya: avocado and papaya salad, 35
pea soup, fresh, 21
peanut butter: vegetable and satay
    salad, 78
pears: warm pears in cider, 90
peppers: lamb's liver with, 40
  mixed pepper pipérade, 73
  red pepper soup with chilli and
    lime, 19
  turkey with yellow pepper sauce, 49
pineapple flambé, 90
pipérade, mixed pepper, 73
pitta breads: quick pitta pizzas, 70
pizzas: French bread pizzas with
    artichokes, 71
  quick pitta pizzas, 70
pork: sweet-and-sour pork, Thai-style, 44
  with marsala and juniper, 43
prawns: chilli prawns, 66
  pan-fried prawns in their shells, 62
  Thai prawn salad, 68
prune and orange pots, 93

R
raspberries: raspberry purée, 13
red fruit filo baskets, 88
red mullet grilled with rosemary, 62
rice: kedgeree with green beans and
    mushrooms, 87
  red fried rice, 86
  seafood pilaff, 56
ricotta: grilled nectarines with spice and, 95
runner beans with tomatoes, 76

S
salade Niçoise, 34
salmon: salmon pasta with parsley sauce, 56
  warm salmon salad, 58
  with watercress sauce, 59
sauces: chocolate, 13
  tomato, 12
scallops with ginger, 66
scone pizza, quick, 12
seafood: seafood pilaff, 56
  spaghetti with seafood sauce, 56
shrimp *see* prawns
smoked haddock: haddock and broccoli
    chowder, 22
smoked mackerel and apple dip, 26
sole: breaded sole batons, 25
spaghetti with seafood sauce, 61
Spanish garlic soup, 20
Spanish-style hake, 60
spinach: poached eggs with, 28
  spinach and beetroot salad, 76
Stilton beefburgers, 37
sweet-and-sour pork, Thai-style, 44

T
tagliatelle: with saffron mussels, 51
  with tomatoes and black olives, 83
techniques, 12–13
Thai prawn salad, 68
tomatoes: fish balls in tomato sauce, 54
  fresh tomato soup with cheese croûtes, 18
  herb omelette with tomato salad, 80
  runner beans with, 76
  tagliatelle with black olives and, 83
  tomato sauce, 12
tuna: salade Niçoise, 34
  summer tuna salad, 32
turkey with yellow pepper sauce, 49

V
veal: ragout of veal, 40
vegetables: pasta with spring vegetables, 85
  vegetable and satay salad, 78

W
watercress: salmon with watercress sauce, 59

Y
yogurt: orange yogurt brûlées, 94

Z
zucchini *see* courgette